THE
COLLEGE CHOICE

A BIBLICAL GUIDE FOR
STUDENTS AND PARENTS

TODD M. SORRELL

**FOREWORDS BY
JOHN MACARTHUR AND STUART SCOTT**

THE
COLLEGE CHOICE

A BIBLICAL GUIDE FOR
STUDENTS AND PARENTS

©2017 by Todd M. Sorrell

ISBN 978-1-936141-39-5

Cover Design by Amelia Schussman

Published by Focus Publishing
PO Box 665
Bemidji, Minnesota 56619

Printed in the United States of America

ENDORSEMENTS

Over the past forty years I have worked as a pastor, counselor and graduate professor, often counseling struggling Christian families who are trying to make good decisions about their child's future education. There is a common problem among families who end up making poor decisions about the education of their children. They see their children graduate from public universities and colleges with a secularized worldview that has undermined their Christian faith. These adult children will often walk away from the church and Christianity. Todd Sorrell has done a masterful job in helping young Christians and their parents see that undergraduate and graduate Christian education is not one option among many equals; rather, that purposeful Christian education is a vital consideration when making the decision about collegiate education. This book should be read by every parent and young person considering where to invest the next four to five years of their resources and lives. It will provide the necessary road map for the right decision that honors Christ.

> **John D. Street**, Chair, Biblical Counseling Graduate
> Programs, The Master's University and Seminary.
> President, Association of Certified Biblical Counselors (ACBC).
> Editor of *Men Counseling Men*; co-author of *The Biblical Counseling Guide for Women*

It has been an enigma to me for years why Christian parents pay a school to shape and influence their children away from the faith they worked so hard to instill. It is as if they are paying to place their children in a lion's den. Yes, secular universities need strong believers, but not impressionable 18 year olds. Todd has thought through this issue well. Christian parents—read this book!

> **Ernie Baker**, Pastor of Counseling, First Baptist Church
> of Jacksonville. Chair of the online BA degree in Biblical
> Counseling, The Master's University. Author of *Marry Wisely, Marry Well*

I rarely hear Christian parents wrestle with the "college decision" as it pertains to the potential spiritual influence—good or bad—that it will have upon their son or daughter. It is not on their radar. They are more inclined to focus initially on academics, scholarships, affordability, or location. I appreciate Todd's consideration given to this important subject. This book will be a great help and resource to every Christian student and parent who reads it!

Shirley Elliott, MABC, The Master's University.
Worship Associate, Christian Family Chapel, Jacksonville, Florida.
Author of *From Heartbroken to Hopeful*

This book makes a very strong case for Christian families to seriously consider sending their believing children to a college which will provide a biblically based worldview and a nurturing spiritual environment, while also offering an excellent education to prepare them for adult responsibilities. Todd Sorrell applies biblical wisdom as he thoroughly analyzes one of the most important decisions a family will ever make.

James Newheiser, Jr., Director of the Christian Counseling Program, Associate Professor of Christian Counseling and Practical Theology at Reformed Theological Seminary Charlotte. Co-author of *Parenting is More than a Formula*

During a time in our nation when worldviews could not be more diametrically opposed, this book reminds us that college is first and foremost about influence. When a commitment of tremendous resources is on the table, it reminds us that Christians have a stewardship with what God has given. When a single four-year period can set the course of an entire life, parents are urged to engage and guide. And when so many options are available, it points out that Christians have a choice, and that choice should not be dictated by the world's value system. In this book, Todd urges young believers and their parents to remember all they have learned about living the Christian life when making the college choice, and to truly make that choice *as Christians*. I recommend this book to any young person, parent, grandparent, or pastor of a young person anticipating the college choice.

Joshua Clutterham, Professor of Bible and Biblical Counseling, Brookes Bible College, St. Louis, MO.
Contributor to *Men Counseling Men*

If you don't get educated through the lens of Scripture,

is that even an education?

—John MacArthur

DEDICATION

This book is dedicated to those who are wondering whether God's Word has anything practical to say about real-life decisions. It does. And the sooner you learn to delight in the Lord, the sooner He will give you the desires of your heart (Psalm 37:4).

And to my wife and children—I thank God for you every day and I pray that we each learn to glorify Him in every decision we make. Even if those decisions seem difficult on this side of eternity.

TABLE OF CONTENTS

FOREWORD
by
John MacArthur

As a pastor of Grace Community Church for nearly fifty years and president of The Master's University and Seminary for over thirty years, I have lived and led in both the academic and church worlds. That experience has convinced me of the critical place of truly Christian education and the need to create an academic experience that honors the Lord by developing a lifetime love for His Word and His church. My goal has always been to equip young people with genuine wisdom based on strong faith in the truth, written and incarnate, and unwavering biblical convictions accompanied by the boldness to live and declare them.

At the same time, as a pastor I have had the challenge of shepherding parents whose children were corrupted by the ungodly influence of both secular universities and compromising, so-called Christian institutions. In both cases, attacks on the truth resulted in serious confusion and loss of conviction. Secular and compromising educational institutions are the most dangerous places intellectually, socially, morally, and spiritually for young people. That is because students are exposed for years to highly developed deceit propagated by clever and educated experts in error. I also know regularly the joy and gratitude of parents whose precious children have grown in grace and spiritual maturity in the Christ-exulting, biblically faithful ministry of The Master's University and The Master's Seminary.

It has been estimated that it takes about sixty to seventy days of repeating or rehearsing patterns of thinking and behavior for them to become habits. We all operate on habits, good or bad, and we struggle to overcome the evil ones. Such are primary obstacles in the way of godliness and virtue. The book of Psalms is the revealed wisdom of God and it begins with a severe warning followed by a rich promise:

How blessed is the man who does not walk in the counsel of the wicked, nor stand in the path of sinners, nor sit in the seat of scoffers! But his delight is in the law of the Lord and in his law he meditates day and night. He will be like a tree *firmly* planted by streams of water, which yields its fruit in its season and its leaf does not wither; and in whatever he does, he prospers. The wicked are not so, but they are like chaff which the wind drives away. Therefore the wicked will not stand in the judgment, nor sinners in the assembly of the righteous. For the Lord knows the way of the righteous, but the way of the wicked will perish. (Psalm 1)

That divine revelation is an educational mandate to all who love the Lord and His Word. No believer can afford to be indifferent to the heavenly demand in this Psalm. The results are too stark—prospering or perishing. Few human experiences have the impact of a college, university, or graduate education because of the length, intensity, and level of exposure. People are the products of their education. For believers, it is only reasonable that those who love the Lord and His Word would desire to be shaped by the truth and not by what is in rebellion to it. In his remarkable book, Todd Sorrell has provided to believers everywhere clarity and an unparalleled direction for making educational choices. Every parent and potential student needs to read this book and heed its biblical wisdom.

John MacArthur, Pastor-teacher of Grace Community Church in Sun Valley, California, president of The Master's University and Seminary, and featured teacher with *Grace to You* media ministry. Author of numerous bestselling books, including *The MacArthur Study Bible, The Gospel According to Jesus,* and *Twelve Ordinary Men.*

FOREWORD
by
Stuart Scott

Decisions. Decisions. When a student stands ready to jump into four years of independence and uncharted territory, this is the necessary guidebook. How do we know what God's will is when it comes to a higher education choice? What biblical and practical principles should a parent and student consider? School choice is a weighty decision that Todd has spoken to clearly and systematically, to help parents and students make a decision they will not regret.

As a college and seminary professor, higher education is where I live. It is surprising how uninformed and unintentional many students are; and how unaware parents can be of what their student is learning, doing, or planning. More importantly, after attending six higher education schools, teaching in three, and having exposure to many more, it is clear to me that not all Christian schools are created equal. And secular institutions—if they cannot be avoided—can be spiritually dangerous places that must be carefully navigated.

One thing is certain. Whether the student is a believer or not, or whether the student chooses a Christian or secular school, wisdom must be applied to achieve the best outcome concerning the higher education experience and one's future vocation. Choices relating to these two are often intertwined. True wisdom, of course, is from above, and found in the pages of the Scriptures. Applying biblical wisdom in decision-making is what pleases Christ and leads always to our good (Colossians 1:9-10).

For both parents and students, Todd asks all the right questions on practical matters, while walking them through scriptural principles that can lead to the wisest school choice. He helps parents think well beyond their own alma mater, beyond a beautiful campus filled with amenities, beyond well-meaning teachers, friendly faculty and staff, beyond the proximity of a school to the student's home, beyond the cost, and even beyond the perceived level of prestige a particular school enjoys. In fact, Todd's goal is to help his readers align their thinking with God's, and he relies on God's own Word to accomplish this. And since the core of this guidebook is to encourage parents and students to do "all things" to the glory of God, get ready to biblically evaluate key heart issues involved in the school choice as well.

With all this and more inside these pages, I know you will find the biblical and practical guidance that drew you to this book. So, go for it, but be ready to have your thinking challenged in this extremely important decision!

> The simple believes everything, but the prudent gives
> thought to his steps (Proverbs 14:15).

> Trust in the Lord with all your heart, and do not
> lean on your own understanding. In all your ways
> acknowledge Him, and He will make straight your paths
> (Proverbs 3:5-6).

Dr. Stuart W. Scott, Professor of Biblical Counseling,
The Master's University. Author of *The Exemplary Husband*

PREFACE

As I will explain in the pages that follow, this has been a difficult book for me to write. I attended public schools through high school and received degrees from two secular universities for college and law school. Only during my biblical counseling studies as an adult at The Master's University did it dawn on me what had been absent from my prior schooling—the blessing and daily application of God's Word throughout my education experience, the learning process, and the classroom setting. While God protected me during those secular years, the world had a significantly greater influence on me than it would have had at a Christian college. God was and remains faithful, but my decision to not involve Him in the college selection process left me with a number of scars that I wish I didn't have.

Having said that, it was not until I began to research and write this book that I began to understand God's intended role in the college selection process. The conclusions set forth in this book are not based on a preconceived notion of where I wanted this research and study to lead. Instead, the Scripture, analysis, and thoughts that I cite fairly represent my journey through God's Word to provide biblical counsel and conclusions that reflect God's holy will. And now I ask you to take that journey with me.

Strangely enough, the issue of college choice raises strong emotions in many people. I have engaged in a number of conversations about this topic and I have found that no matter how softly I peddle the issue and my conclusions, people get very defensive about it—especially when they already have chosen a college or their kids are in or already have graduated from a secular school. To cut those emotions off before they take root and before an objective analysis of God's Word is conducted, let me say this: I am not saying that any particular college choice is a sin, nor am I saying that any particular college choice is pleasing to God. That judgment is God's alone and can vary among believers, depending on how those choices are made. What I am saying is that God desires that you voluntarily involve Him in the decision and He wants you to submit to His will in the final choice. And the best way to do that is to decide—in advance—to do His will even before you are sure what it might involve. Even in the college choice.

INTRODUCTION

Let's get one thing straight. There is no one correct answer when picking a college and despite what some colleges might have you believe, Jesus' first stop upon his return will not be at a specific campus. God did not see fit to provide a list of acceptable colleges, nor can anyone specifically identify the precise college for a parent or child to select. However, the absence of a precise command on the subject does not mean that the Bible is silent on the issue. Even though He did not dedicate a chapter in the Bible to college choice, God has much to say about the subject. As with most issues believers face today, all God's children need to do is search the Scriptures for guidance in this important decision. When people seek God diligently, they *will* find Him (Proverbs 8:17) and His wisdom (James 1:5). This book seeks to provide clear biblical counsel on the issue of college choice. The real question is this: "Will you follow that counsel?"

In order to answer that question in the affirmative, the believer must first understand that every decision has eternal consequences. Indeed, many significant obstacles in the Christian life may be traced back to a failure to make that connection; each choice relating to values, actions, thinking, and where and how one will spend time and resources relates to and reflects one's commitment to follow Christ. With regard to education, too many Christians seem to think that choosing a college has nothing to do with their faith. They do not view the decision as a "heart" issue. In fact, this most common experience does not involve spiritual considerations or even input from pastors or fellow believers. Parents and students alike have conformed to the pattern of this world when making a college choice, and even if they do afford a passing spiritual thought, they tend to believe that the decision is spiritually neutral. They are wrong.

Specifically, the Bible speaks directly to the heart issues involved in college choice, and Scripture is totally sufficient for the believer who desires to know God's will for how and where he should spend the college years (2 Peter 1:3; 2 Timothy 3:15-17). Although to a student it may feel like college is toward the tail end of the journey, it is an important part of the education process and is often the first time a young person is living apart from the immediate shelter and guidance of his parents. The college experience involves an extended period when a student's heart will be filled *without* engaging in daily interaction with his family. Whenever he goes, he will be learning (i.e., filling his mind; see Colossians 2:8). The primary "filling" of his mind will occur in a classroom by people neither he nor his parents have ever met. In fact, the whole point of college is to be influenced. Should a Christian student be sitting at the feet of those who ignore or scoff at the Word of God, or does God desire another path? Is the overall college experience to be considered alongside the actual vocational skills that will be acquired? Also, college is not typically free, so whatever choice is made, money that God has entrusted to the believing parent should be used wisely and to His glory. In short, if the focus of a believer's life is to know God and make Him known (and to enjoy Him forever), how does a college choice advance or distract from that goal?

There also are a number of practical considerations. For example, what options are available to the student and which of those options would most glorify God? Do those options include a Christian college? A secular college?

- What if the student does not want to attend a Christian college?

- What if he is not a believer?

- What if he has a specialized focus that is not offered at a Christian college (e.g., "I want to be a pilot" or play "big time" college athletics)?

- What if the Christian college actually costs *more* than a secular institution?

- What if the student does not believe he will be intellectually challenged at anything other than a top-ranked secular university?

- What if a parent refuses to pay for a Christian education?

- What if the parents disagree with one another on college choice?

- What if the student already is enrolled in a secular college?

Does God's Word have anything to say about these questions and the decision-making process? Of course it does. God's desire is that this decision (like all decisions) be reached through the filter of God's written Word and with the goal of spiritual maturity in mind. If one type of school seeks to honor self, and the other seeks to honor God by cultivating thoughts and behaviors guided by Scripture, the believer would do well to consider the selection in advance of making a final decision. As Plato said, "What is honored in a country is cultivated there."[1] Applying that to education, the question is this: What will be cultivated during your college years?

Biblical counsel in this regard has great potential to impact the sanctification process of those involved in the decision. Perhaps their lives seem relatively comfortable, and they "feel" like things are going just fine. However, having a discussion about college selection has the potential to bring numerous people into the Word of God who might not be making the connection between the Bible and practical decisions. Digging into the Scriptures on this particular point might be the encouragement those same people need to start consulting Scripture in everyday decisions, thus aligning their lives with God's plan. It might even encourage young people to start considering how their school and career choices should be impacted by God's plan for their lives, which must be focused on Jesus Christ. And, of course, impacting even one person in this regard might put him in the environment where he can grow and learn about the loving Creator of the universe who wants to have a relationship with him.

The need is evident. I have looked far and wide and there is very little practical, biblical advice written for parents or college bound students in terms of where they should go and where God's money should be spent. Many have adopted the world's decision-making process on

---

1 Plato, *Republic, Book VIII,* trans. Benjamin Jowett (1892), annot. David Trumbull (Agathan Ass. 2009), accessed October 6, 2015, http://www.bostonleadershipbuilders.com/plato/republic/book8.htm.

this topic, some have agreed to participate in the world's folly for four years, and others have simply resigned themselves to try to survive the college experience in a school they might not have chosen had they first sought biblical counsel on the subject. However, education is not something to be "survived," like war; instead, it should be nourishing, like a well-planned meal. After all, no one is supposed to just "survive" a meal.[2] The world, on the other hand, offers a seemingly infinite supply of information and promotional materials on how to choose the "right" school. Since biblical counsel seeks to bridge the gap between what one believes and how one lives (or, in biblical terms, making sure one is both a hearer and a doer), and since college often purports to teach both, it is time to counsel believers about the heart issues associated with such a decision.[3]

---

2 *See* Douglas Wilson, *Why Christian Kids Need a Christian Education* (Monroe, LA: Athanasius Press, 2013), 18.

3 Much of this discussion can—and perhaps should—relate to education from birth through high school, and the principles included herein are not limited to the college experience. It could be argued that these principles apply even more strongly to younger students who are more easily influenced. However, since there are a number of works already in existence on the issue of elementary, high school, and home school education, the decision was made to limit this discussion to college choice since there is very little scholarship on this point.

CHAPTER 1

WHAT IS COLLEGE?

For purposes of this book, the words "college" and "university" will be used interchangeably and refer to a four-year, residential, post-high school institution, typical in the United States. Although there are exceptions, the typical college experience involves living in student housing, being instructed in courses relevant to one's primary course of study, participating in extra-curricular activities and organizations, and meeting new people. So from that perspective, answering the question, "What is college?" is a relatively simple task.

However, college is not merely a building of brick and mortar and well-read textbooks. It is a place where the minds of students are molded by professors, books, friends, organizations, experiences, and opportunities. It is a four-year period where students are encouraged to focus on and acquire skills for lifelong jobs. It is a time of maturation for many students who have never lived apart from their parents. It is a time when deep friendships are formed and spouses are often met.

But college is even more than that. Through the work of the Holy Spirit, the college years represent an opportunity to transition from teenage foolishness to wise adult living. Beliefs that were inculcated during childhood are hardened or rejected. New ideas are presented and considered. Religious beliefs mature from family values to personal commitments, or are replaced by faith in something (or someone) else. In short, college is a place and time where morality is developed alongside vocational skills. For the Christian, it is a period of time when God graciously extends the opportunity to know and serve Him. And while this four-year period is marked most notably by training and influence, it is the combination of these factors that combine to form an overall college experience that impacts and shapes almost every aspect of the rest of an individual's life. It *is* that important.

Training

Formal college training typically is provided through a student's primary course of study (his "major"). There are a variety of routes for choosing a major, and there is no one "right" way to do it. Some students arrive at college already having selected a major in light of a laser-beam focus they have had since childhood. They have a particular interest and are intent on pursuing it. They often narrow college options by first determining whether a school offers such a program and then deciding which program is best. Others enter college thinking they will major in a particular field, then change course after discovering that the subject matter is of no interest to them. (Some have this decision made for them by their inability to keep up with the rigor of the course requirements.) Finally, there are those who pursue courses of study that just fit with their schedules or lives. Some of these individuals have no particular interest in the fields they ultimately choose, but they simply want to obtain a degree, either for a résumé or for post-graduate studies.

The idea behind having a primary course of study is to engage in focused learning in a particular field as preparation for life's work. An engineering student might be taught mathematical concepts to assist in the calculations he someday will be required to perform when designing a bridge. A student majoring in linguistics may learn how dialects are formed and developed, which will assist him while he serves as a translator for the United Nations. A communications major might learn how mass media affects purchasing decisions, a very important concept in his post-graduate advertising job. And a biblical studies major will learn to understand, interpret, and apply biblical literature, which he can use in church leadership, personal Bible study, and everyday life. In short, *learning* has historically been the primary purpose of attending college.

For a believer, learning is related directly to serving God. Once a Christian narrows his vocational pursuit based on a clear reading of Scripture, an objective analysis of his abilities and opportunities, a consideration of his personal desires, and in consultation with mature believers, he then should evaluate the most effective way to prepare for that service. College training is an integral step in that process.

Influence and the Overall College Experience

Formal classroom training is not the only ingredient that makes up the four-year college journey. The overall college experience is a conflux of factors, including studies, faculty influence, peer relationships, content, social activities, peripheral pursuits, and religious involvement. Much like a valley where numerous strong rivers converge to morph and form a rugged or beautiful downstream landscape, the impact of these different influences during college cannot be overstated and none should be considered in isolation.

School Authority Figures are Part of the College Experience

As will be discussed at various points throughout this book, college is a time to be influenced. That influence begins in the classroom, as described above, where students are taught core concepts relating to their fields of study. But influence during the college years involves much more than book learning. Professors, for example, can teach a student literature, but also can influence a student's belief about that literature. In fact, a number of Old Testament passages often are assigned reading in secular literature courses, but they are not taught as conveying historical truth. A professor who admires the writing style of the book of Job, for example, but who mocks those who believe the story will have an influence on a student sitting under his tutelage. Similarly, a professor who holds the Bible in high esteem and who teaches it as a reliable, historical document will influence his listeners in that direction. In addition to their teaching philosophies, professors who show great care for students and who get students excited about learning also wield great influence. In fact, many students cite to such interactions as having strong, positive influences on their lives and jobs, well into the future (Proverbs 13:20).[4]

Content Is Part of the College Experience

In addition to faculty members, students are influenced by the material to which they are exposed and the assignments they are given. A history

---

4 Julie Ray and Stephanie Kafka, "Life in College Matters for Life After College," *Gallup*, accessed January 28, 2016, http://www.gallup.com/poll/168848/life-college-matters-life-college.aspx.

student required to read and analyze the United States Constitution might come away with a sense of awe as he considers the social and historical environment in which it was crafted. In a negative sense, a student required to read pornographic literature might have his mind opened to perversions he might not otherwise have considered, leading to struggles in his thought life that were not present before. And a science student who reads about the miraculous metamorphosis of the caterpillar-butterfly may be blown away by God's creativity, as well as the inherent contradictions even that one transformation places on the theory of evolution.[5] Information absorbed during college powerfully impacts one's thinking and conduct (Proverbs 4:23).

Peers are Part of the College Experience

The college experience does not stop with the influences of training, faculty, or information. Just as in all educational experiences leading up to college, friends have a huge impact on a student's thoughts, affections, goals, and conduct. "Peer pressure" has long been stigmatized as a negative (and often is associated with immoral or risky behavior), but it also can be positive, depending on the character of the friends and the pressure being placed on the student (*see, e.g.,* Proverbs 12:26; 13:20; 1 Corinthians 15:33). Likewise, campus organizations to which a student belongs can provide contact with like-minded students and leaders and can present opportunities for extra-curricular experiences that may influence a student's perspective on community service, outreach, and hobbies. Friends often lead a student to join such organizations, and some of them involve lifelong associations, such as fraternities, scholarly groups, and environmental organizations. The impact of a student's social life and relationships with his peers during college should not be underestimated.

Peripheral School Pursuits and Involvement are Part of the College Experience

Student life is not limited to the campus. Studies have shown that internship and job opportunities during college have a great impact on a student's well-being after college. Specifically, students who hold

---

5 Richard William Nelson, "Darwin Then and Now," *DarwinThenandNow.com*, accessed January 29, 2016, http://www.darwinthenandnow.com/2010/08/butterfly-nightmare/.

internships or jobs where they are able to apply what they learn in the classroom report a high correlation between that activity and life satisfaction after college.[6] Put another way, connecting book learning to practical living influences a student's outlook on life.

Peripheral pursuits might also involve activities such as studying abroad or engaging in long-term projects. Studying abroad, for example, may prompt a student to love foreign languages or become interested in a new culture. A long-term project might direct a student into an area he might not otherwise have considered. Suffice it to say that the elements that constitute a college experience vary as widely as the students enrolling in college, as well as the opportunities presented to them, and each of these factors has the potential to ignite new passions and interests in a student.

Family and Religious Connections are Part of the College Experience

Finally, connection to family and church during the college years has a great influence on a student's life. A student who remains connected to a caring family will continue to care what his family thinks about his studies, his accomplishments, and his character. Likewise, being involved in a local church and submitting to the authority of the pastor/elders (as well as Scripture) plays an important role in a young person's life during these four years.[7] For the Christian, this involvement is not an option; it is a command and for the believer's own good and God's glory (Hebrews 10:25; 13:17; Romans 8:28-29; 1 Corinthians 10:31). This outward conduct, in addition to the inward surrender to Christ, is perhaps the most important influence on a believer's life during the college years and should not be dismissed as an afterthought.

---

6 Ray, "Life in College Matters for Life After College."

7 Of the Protestant clergy, thirty-eight percent of youth pastors and thirty-six percent of senior pastors frequently discuss college plans with their students. *See* McKinley Cobb "Teen Dreams: Church Influences Career Choice," *Crosswalk.com*, accessed January 30, 2016, http://www.crosswalk.com/family/parenting/teens/teenage-dreams.html.

College Is Community

There is no other way to put it. College is a community experience. At the inception of a student's college years, he will be inserting himself into an established community, and then will spend the next four years developing his own community that will be as big or as small as his energy and interests permit. It might involve a small group of roommates, or it might be as large as the entire school. It might include an athletic team, or it might revolve around religious student organizations. It might stem from his specific field of study, or it might expand to include those in his general education or elective courses. Whatever the makeup, a student will seek to fit into his chosen community by participating in classroom discussions and group activities. He will develop relationships and engage in pursuits with or through the group. He will take classes and eat meals in a community setting. He will listen to conversations and add to them. Although there is no specifically defined community for each student, each will be a community member. It is an unavoidable and integral part of the four-year college experience.

With all of this in mind, it is easy to see that a comprehensive college experience involves far more than a textbook or single professor. It is a four-year series of interactions, choices, relationships, circumstances, and influences that the student will experience in a chosen community at a specific location during a precise moment in history. This is college.

CHAPTER 2

THE COLLEGE CONVERSATION
AND TYPICAL CONSIDERATIONS

Little Johnny isn't so little anymore. In fact, he is a strapping 18-year-old man finishing up high school and ready to select a college. Even though Johnny is not keen to write more than one essay for his college applications, Johnny sets about the task of selecting schools he might like to attend. For the first time in what seems like forever, he asks his parents for a bit of advice (even if he intends to ignore it). They put their heads together and the conversation goes something like this:

Johnny: Mom, Dad, my school counselor tells me it's time to apply for college.

Dad: Well, you'll go to State, of course. That's where I went. Go Sandbuilders!

Johnny: Yeah, I guess. But some of my friends are going to apply to Widepath University. I hear it's a good school. I don't want to go to a place where I don't know anyone.

Mom: University! Oh, my son. I'm so proud! You'll be a doctor or lawyer before you know it. [Crying, she wraps her arms around his neck as he grimaces and tries to squirm away.]

Johnny: Aww, Mom. Please don't cry on me again. Sheesh. Anyway, I don't really know what I want to do yet. But Widepath University has a lot of majors I can choose from. I hear that there's a cool, new "gender studies" major that is pretty easy. [He pushes his mother away.]

Dad: Gender studies!?! What in the…? Well, anyway, that school sounds kind of expensive. But let's say you go there. Then what?

Johnny: Then I get a job. That's what.

Mom: A job! It sounds so grown up!

Dad: Anyway, as I was saying, it's settled then. You will apply to both schools and see which one accepts you. Both have solid reputations, both offer a lot of degrees, and they're close enough so you can come home to visit once in a while. I figure they'll both put me in the poorhouse, but I guess that's my job.

Johnny: Thanks, Dad. College is going to be so much fun. I hear that Widepath University has a bunch of fraternities and they have an annual underwear 5k run and the tailgating at the football games is off the charts!

Dad: But you'll be studying—right? I'm not sending you to school just so you can party for four years.

Johnny: Oh yeah, of course. I mean, that's why I'm going, right? To study.

Mom: Underwear run?

That is the end of the discussion and (quite often) the end of the analysis. Although the above conversation is imaginary and designed to highlight one extreme scenario, it is not complete fiction. In fact, this conversation or some variation of it is played out repeatedly throughout the western world, sometimes spanning days, weeks, or even months. Sometimes it is a single parent talking to a child; sometimes it is the mom who is firmer about the finances and studies; and sometimes the child has a more focused outlook on his studies and career. But the gist of the thinking is the same. College is something to be experienced (or at least survived), and the almost parallel considerations of prestige, debt, and social activities often dominate the student's thought process. This is the world's pattern.[8]

---

8 As will be discussed herein, a Christian family's conversation might be a bit different, but it might just as easily revolve around academic reputation, big time college athletics, or price.

More specifically, a recent secular survey asked approximately 200,000 college freshmen to rate which factors were "very important" in influencing their college choice. They were allowed to choose as many of the factors as they wanted in their responses. The results are ranked in descending order:

1. College has very good academic reputation (63.8%)

2. This college's graduates get good jobs (55.9%)

3. I was offered financial assistance (45.6%)

4. The cost of attending this college (43.3%)

5. A visit to this campus (41.8%)

6. College has a good reputation for its social activities (40.2%)

7. Wanted to go to a college about this size (38.8%)

8. College's grads get into top grad/professional schools (32.8%)

9. The percentage of students that graduate from this college (30.4%)

10. I wanted to live near home (20.1%)

11. Information from a website (18.7%)

12. Rankings in national magazines (18.2%)

13. Parents wanted me to go to this school (15.1%)

14. Admitted early decision and/or early action (13.7%)

15. Could not afford first choice (13.4%)

16. High school counselor advised me (10.3%)

17. Not offered aid by first choice (9.5%)

18. Athletic department recruited me (8.9%)

19. Attracted by the religious affiliation/orientation of college (7.4%)

20. My relatives wanted me to come here (6.8%)

21. My teacher advised me (6.8%)

22. Private college counselor advised me (3.8%)

23. Ability to take online courses (3.2%)[9]

While these results are not surprising given that the world has suppressed the truth of God (Romans 1:18), they are rather telling. Reputation, jobs, cost, and social activities rank far higher than religious considerations. Even parental preference is over halfway down the list. This survey indicates that the world's pattern in choosing colleges is focused on perceived worldly prestige, earning and saving money, and having fun. Serving, knowing, and glorifying God have almost zero to do with this decision. Why is that? The answer lies in something called "worldview."[10]

---

9 Kathy Wyer, "Survey: More freshmen than ever say they go to college to get better jobs, make more money - The American Freshman: National Norms Fall 2012," *Higher Education Research Institute,* accessed December 31, 2014, http://www.heri.ucla.edu/pr-display. php?prQry=111; *see also* Ruth Sims, "New research on student emotions in college choice: Part 1," *Noel-Levitz,* accessed December 31, 2014, http://blog.noellevitz.com/2014/08/28/ new-research-student-emotions-college-choice-part-1/.

10 Sadly, the above experience seems fairly typical of *both* the Christian and non-Christian. In other words, many Christians have conformed to the world's thinking and practice when it comes to choosing a college. Other than brief lip service, many believers do not allow spiritual considerations to impact school choice. Sure, they might discuss Christian organizations on campus and the really spiritual ones may even look up a few churches in the area, but godliness in a school, the morality of its curriculum, or the beliefs of its faculty are rarely considered, especially when analyzed in conjunction with the spiritual maturity of the believing students who are charged with making the decision.

CHAPTER 3

WORLDVIEW

WHAT IS A WORLDVIEW AND WHY DOES IT MATTER?

A worldview is the lens through which one views life and the world.[11] Such an interpretative lens helps people make sense of things and make decisions. The word "worldview" is derived from the German term, *Weltanschauung,* and refers to a cluster of beliefs a person holds about important issues such as morality, origins, consequences, and eternity.[12] It provides a framework by which individuals interpret and evaluate reality and, thus, is the orientation of the heart. The assumptions forming a worldview can be entirely true, entirely false, or a combination of the two. Everyone has a worldview and it colors every evaluation, value, and decision.

A viable worldview provides answers to questions such as whether God exists; where people came from; how people can actually know anything; how people should live; what values people should have and why; whether humanity has a fundamental problem and, if so, whether it can be solved; the meaning and purpose of life; and whether there is life after death.[13]

Although there are thousands of religious and other beliefs ascribed to today, they can be reduced to a handful of helpful categories. For example, there are naturalists—people who believe in natural causes for everything, that the material world is all that exists, and who

---

11 *See generally* Phillip Johnson, foreword to *Total Truth,* by Nancy Pearcey (Wheaton, IL: Crossway Books, 2005), 11.

12 Kenneth Samples, "What in the World is a Worldview?" *Reasons to Believe,* accessed January 6, 2015, http://www.reasons.org/articles/what-in-the-world-is-a-worldview; *see also* John MacArthur, "Introduction," in *Think Biblically*, edited by John MacArthur (Wheaton, IL: Crossway, 2003), 13.

13 Ibid.; *see also* James Sire, "8 Questions Every Worldview Must Answer," *Christianity. com*, accessed January 6, 2015, http://www.christianity.com/theology/other-religions-be-liefs/8-questions-every-worldview-must-answer.html?p=0.

discount the supernatural or spiritual. There are pantheists—those who believe that the spiritual dimension is all that exists, and that everything else is an illusion. There are spiritualists/polytheists—those who believe in thousands (or more) of gods or spirits, and that everything that occurs is a result of spiritual influence on the material world. There are postmodernists—people who believe that truth is relative to one's culture. And there are theists—people who believe in an infinite, personal God who sets objective moral standards, in a universe that is both material and spiritual, and in the fact that the world had a beginning and will have an end.[14]

In light of the above, it is not difficult to see that our worldview will impact how we make decisions and prioritize values. Someone who believes truth is relative to one's culture will have a far different perspective on human sexuality and morals than one who believes in a perfect God who has laid down one objective, moral standard for all to follow. Put another way, the postmodernist will value tolerance for different sexual practices and preferences, while the theist will esteem conformity to God's law. Likewise, a person who believes spiritual beings are behind every event will have a different take on an earthquake than a naturalist, who does not believe in the spiritual world. One (the pantheist) will be more prone to spend money on altars and gifts to appease the spirits, while the other (the naturalist) may invest in earthquake retrofitting for his old house. Worldviews matter because they color how we interpret the world and events and, thus, impact the decisions we make.

What Is a Christian Worldview?

There are two types of worldviews that are considered "Christian." But let's be clear. One of these is not really Christian if, by that term, one means a worldview that a true follower of Christ should have. Specifically, there is the person who claims to be a Christian, yet who does not think much about spiritual matters. At a minimum, his "Christianity" does not impact his thinking in everyday decisions. Sure, he claims to trust in Jesus for salvation, but whatever faith he has seems to be limited to those things that are clearly spiritual or

14 Dennis McCallum, "Five Worldviews," *Xenos Christian Fellowship*, accessed January 6, 2015, http://www.xenos.org/classes/papers/5wldview.htm.

religious. His version of God is just not that interested in the mundane. This person sees much of his life as spiritually "neutral."

Then there is the Christian who believes in an almighty, sovereign Creator who made humans in the image of God (Genesis 1:26-28; Psalm 104; Psalm 115:3). This person knows that God loved him enough to send His Son to die in his place, and who desires a personal relationship with him. This Christian sees his purpose on this earth to know God, to make Him known to others, and to bring glory to God. His divine calling as a disciple of Christ is pervasive and he allows that perspective to dictate his life's direction in all areas. He trusts God in all things and looks forward to an eternity with Him. There is joy in obeying God's commands, even if not always easy. He has made an oath and confirmed it, to keep God's righteous rules (Psalm 119:106). His worldview and theology lead him to understand that every thought and action can and should be an act of worship and, in fact, he considers every decision in life to be an opportunity to please God (1 Corinthians 10:31). He understands that he was made to do good works to the glory of God and because of Him (Ephesians 2:10). At its core, the Christian worldview is filtered with the understanding that there is a wide gate that leads to destruction and a narrow gate that leads to heaven for those who find it (Matthew 7:13-14). And while it is God who seeks after and initiates the process with believers (John 4:23), it is also clear that each individual—in order to find the gate—should be looking for it since God will be found by those who seek Him (Jeremiah 29:13; Deuteronomy 4:29; Matthew 6:33). And those who seek Him will enter through the true gate—Jesus Christ— through the power of the Holy Spirit (John 10:7, 9).

How Does Your Worldview Impact College Choice?

Against that backdrop, individual worldviews have an enormous impact on college choice and, necessarily, the comprehensive college experience that one seeks. The secular worldview—which, unfortunately, seems to be the one often adopted by both believers and non-believers alike when choosing colleges—tends to color the decision with self-centered desires, outward appearance, worldly success, and financial considerations. For this reason, the top ten factors identified above by hundreds of thousands of recent college freshmen include things like academic reputation, jobs, cost, and social activities. A secular worldview devoid of spiritual considerations does not have a God-centered lens through which to analyze the choice. "If there is no God—or at least one who is not interested in the details of my college choice—then there is no reason to bring him into the mix. I'll just make my decision based on what I want and value."

There are at least two reasons why believers might employ the secular worldview when choosing colleges. First, many people who sit in Sunday pews do very little critical analysis when it comes to college choice. For example, many Christian parents attended secular schools and they want/expect their children to do the same.[15] After all, "it was good enough for me, so it's good enough for my kid. I didn't turn out so bad." They are most comfortable when their children attire themselves in the same type of Christianity that they wear, which is reserved mostly for Sundays. They rarely, if ever, consider the biblical command to "examine yourselves, to see whether you are in the faith" (2 Corinthians 13:5). Their Christianity is fairly superficial, so God is left out of the equation.[16] They do not rely on the Bible as a resource when considering post-high school education.

Second, many Christians (by word or deed) believe that much of education is neutral.[17] According to this way of thinking, college choice is not a spiritual event; it has no moral element. At best, it is purely vocational. The "god" of this thinking is not interested in such trivial, non-spiritual matters. Again, these individuals have not labored over Scripture to analyze God's thinking on the subject.

But neutrality is not an option for a Bible-believing Christian. Evil is the absence of good.[18] Indeed, even choosing a "lesser" good is corrupt and, therefore, evil. God Himself warned that the "lukewarm" will be vomited from His mouth (Revelation 3:20). There is no such

---

15 *See* Wilson, *Why Christian Kids Need a Christian Education*, 10.

16 As an acquaintance of mine once said when he decided to leave our church, "Too many people here take their Christianity too seriously."

17 Wilson, *Why Christian Kids Need a Christian Education*, 9.

18 Greg Koukl, "Augustine on Evil," *Stand to Reason*, accessed October 5, 2015, http://www.str.org/articles/augustine-on-evil#.VLNZ8otyc20, *citing* Augustine, *The City of God*, XI, Chap. 9.

thing as a neutral decision or attitude. It is either done to the glory of God, or it is not (Colossians 3:17).[19] The former is good; the latter is evil. Christians have been set free from the bondage of sin and they should celebrate their freedom by including God in every decision by applying biblical principles to each one. Not doing so is a return to a godless way of thinking. Put another way, making a college choice without considering God is sin (the way of the world), just as is deciding what to look at on the Internet without considering God's commands, or choosing to eat a snack without regard to God's glory. In short, all good things come from Him, and His children should be grateful and worshipful in all things (James 1:17; Psalm 118:24; Colossians 3:17; *see also* Romans 1:21). When God said, "Whether you eat or drink, or whatever you do, do all to the glory of God" (1 Corinthians 10:31), He knew exactly what He was saying. Everything—whether mundane or monumental—should be done with His glory in mind. Failure to do so is a violation of a clear command of Scripture.[20]

For a Christian who seeks to follow God's commands in his entire life, his worldview provides a God-colored lens that will color every decision. God wants all things done to His glory, so the Christian will seek to understand how choosing a college can bring glory to God. God is the provider of all good things, including children, money, and time, so the Christian will seek to discern where these gifts should be employed. God is a personal God, bestowing unique talents and interests on every individual, so the Christian will seek to glorify God by discovering where his intelligence will best be developed and how those interests will be guided into God-glorifying activities. He will consult Scripture, seek wise counsel, consider his circumstances and personal desires, and employ common sense, all in an effort to determine God's individual will for his life.[21] In short, the Christian

---

19 "There is nothing in our experience, however trivial, worldly, or even evil, which cannot be thought about christianly. There is likewise nothing in our experience, however sacred, which cannot be thought about secularly." Harry Blamires, *The Christian Mind* (London: Holy Trinity Church, 1963), 45.

20 Notably, many Christians do not recognize that sin can even be inadvertent. The flesh is so deceptive that even believers have "hidden" faults underneath the layers of presumptuous sins (Psalm 19:12-13). As such, God's children must carefully examine every decision to ensure that it affirmatively chooses to place God first.

21 Gary Friesen, *Decision Making and the Will of God* (Portland, OR: Multnomah Press, 1980), 49.

worldview absolutely will impact the decision to choose a college, whether for oneself or for one's child.

Of course, this still does not answer the question of "where" one should go to school. Just that God should be in the decision and that His written Word should be consulted for guidance.

CHAPTER 4

THE PURPOSE OF COLLEGE

WHAT IT IS NOT (OR WHAT IT *SHOULD NOT* BE)

While there are numerous factors that contribute to, influence, and enhance the overall college experience, becoming "educated" is the primary and historical reason that colleges exist. Since God should be involved in the choice of a college for a Christian, it would be helpful to know what He says about education and, more specifically, this four-year experience. This, like all other trails in this book, leads back to Scripture, which contains the very words of God (2 Timothy 3:16). It is helpful, however, to begin with an explanation of what college is not.

College Should Not Lead a Student to Embrace Everything Presented to Him

Pursuing an education and participating in the overall college experience is not an opportunity to be foolishly open-minded to the point of dishonoring God. Although some may argue that there is a "time for everything" (Ecclesiastes 3:1), there is never good occasion to sin (Romans 6:12). Indeed, believers are called to holy living, even during the college years (1 Peter 1:15-16).

College Should Not Require a Student to Subject Himself to Evil

The college experience is not a time to subject oneself to evil, influential teaching. Mankind should not only refuse to be led astray by those who scorn God's precepts (Proverbs 12:26), but one also must take care to not become scoffers by practice or attitude. As the psalmist articulates, "blessed is the man who walks not in the counsel of the wicked, nor stands in the way of sinners, nor sits in the seat of scoffers" (Psalm 1:1-3; *see also* Psalm 26:4-5). If enticed to sin, believers must not consent (Proverbs 1:10). They are to "hate the assembly of evildoers" (Psalm 26:5). As discussed in more detail below, much of the typical college experience and much of what passes for education today is wicked, does not please God, and should never be entertained by believers (Habakkuk 1:13; Psalm 5:4; 1 Thessalonians 5:22).

College Should Not Be Self-Centered

The college experience should be selfless, not self-centered (2 Timothy 4:3). This point can be divided into two categories. A self-centered experience or education can be sinful because it seeks personal glory, advancement, or accumulation.[22] Or, it can also prove sinful when the self-centeredness simply omits God and encourages independence from the Creator. Wicked people "renounce God" and proclaim that He is an absentee deity who will never call to account (Psalm 10:13). They rely on their own tongues for victory since, as they say, no one "is master over us" (Psalm 12:4). Their arrogant speech restricts the good they will experience to this life (Psalm 17:10, 14), and the consequences for those who demand their independence will be severe (Psalm 2:1-5, those who seek to be free from God will be broken and dashed as God terrifies them in His fury; *see also* Psalm 73:18-19). In short, since all human endeavors should have as their object the glory of God (1 Corinthians 10:31), the four-year college experience must also follow suit.

College Should Not Isolate Believers from God's Instruments of Sanctification

A student's four-year college experience should not be isolating. Modern-day studies can be overwhelming. They can be so intense and time-consuming that a student is drawn into studying (and learning) solo. The perceived reward for academic success can make extra-curricular activities seem dispensable. However, the Christian student must not fall into the trap of isolating himself from God's corporate instruments of sanctification, such as consistent Christian fellowship

---

22 *See generally* T.M. Moore, "Losing your way on the path to wisdom," The Chuck Colson Center for Christian Worldview, accessed April 21, 2015, http://www.colsoncenter. org/the-center/columns/viewpoint/22810-losing-your-way-on-the-path-to-wisdom (using Solomon as an example of one who took his eyes off the Lord as "the exclusive end and focus of all his life and learning," and as one who did not give God glory for all that he had learned and achieved).

and involvement in a local church (Hebrews 10:25). Not only must a believing student practice personal spiritual disciplines (Bible reading, prayer, worship, fasting, etc.), but he also must not become so busy that he disregards the Body of Christ (Romans 12:4-5). The local church is where one commits to the practices that will stimulate "love and good works" (Hebrews 10:24). As such, not only should a student seek wise counsel in selecting a school, but he also must remain connected to that counsel and to the Body of Christ throughout his studies. In short, no one should assume that a school faculty is wholly responsible for teaching and stirring individuals to personal holiness. Such a pattern of living must be fostered in the local church (and also by parents), even during the college years. Indeed, God's definition of education would never require personal isolation, separated from the Body of Christ.

So, if a college experience should not foster foolish thinking, if its content should be free from influential, wicked teaching and activities, if it should not encourage self-centered living, and if it should not isolate believers from God's instruments of righteousness, what is the purpose of a four-year college experience, and what counsel does the Bible provide for those who wish to understand God's desire in the learning process?

What It Is (or What It *Should* Be)

God commands believers to "see to it that no one takes you captive by philosophy and empty deceit, according to human tradition, according to the elemental spirits of the world, and not according to Christ" (Colossians 2:8). Since the goal is to avoid human principles and follow Christ, then God's Word must be consulted to determine what He has to say about education and the college experience.

College Should Equip ("College Is Not Camp")

Do not discount the advice set forth herein by characterizing it as impractical and unrealistic. You might interpret this description of college as some sort of camp experience, a moral training ground where friendships and activities are pursued instead of skills and knowledge sufficient to engage in a lifelong trade or profession. But make no mistake. God is just as interested in His children redeeming their time during college as He is while they are in church or on a job or on vacation (Proverbs 12:11; 13:4; Colossians 3:23). Indeed, Scripture directs people to number *each* of their days and to walk in wisdom: "Look carefully then how you walk, not as unwise but as wise, making the best use of the time, because the days are evil" (Ephesians 5:15-16). There is no exception for the college years.

With God's exhortations in mind, it is easy to grasp the concept that an education worth pursuing is one that equips believers for future service. Although a student's future may involve a full-time position in Christian ministry, that service might just as easily result in a lengthy tenure as a math teacher, a career as a lawyer, or working as an engineer. A believer with an aptitude and God-given desire for accounting should not view his college years as a four-year break from honing his accounting skills and knowledge. In fact, while employers want to hire hard-working, honest, and discerning individuals, they typically will not choose candidates who lack the corresponding job skills required for the positions available. So while the college experience—like all pursuits—does provide an opportunity for moral training and discipline, it also should be designed to prepare the student for the hard work and excellence in craft that please God, that tend to influence others to hold believers in high regard, and that provide for daily necessities and generous giving (1 Thessalonians 3:10-12; Ephesians 4:28). In sum, you are not going to camp (college) to party with your friends and take a break from life. You're going to learn new skills, to influence others and to be influenced, and to grow in Christ-likeness.

College Should Be Based on Biblical Principles

Whether in college or beyond, believers are not called *solely* to hone vocational skills. They also are called to use reason (Proverbs 27:17), to pursue wise counsel (Proverbs 12:15; 15:22), and to surround themselves with other believers (1 Thessalonians 5:11; Hebrews 10:25). Just as biblical doctrine must be conveyed through sound teaching (2 Timothy 4:3), there is no reason to believe that God would condone the teaching of false or twisted information in any context, including at college. In fact, if knowledge is the goal, the "fear of the

Lord" is the key ingredient (*see* Proverbs 1:7, "The fear of the Lord is the beginning of knowledge; fools despise wisdom and instruction"). A college experience that is pleasing to God must be God-centered. An education and college experience that promotes selfish ambition, human-centered thinking, or perverse ideology comes from the darkness of hell-bound demons and the unregenerate human heart. Indeed, since the blessed man is the one who finds delight in God's Word (Psalm 1:2; 26:4-5), implicit in the promise that such a man will be firm in the faith, will yield spiritual fruit, and will prosper in God's eyes is the idea that anti-biblical teaching and influences may undermine those goals (Psalm 1:2-3). Accordingly, education and the overall college experience should arise from or be undergirded by biblical principles.[23]

College Should Foster Discernment

The purpose of education, like all human activity, is to align one's thinking with that of God (Philippians 4:8; Romans 8:5-6; 12:2; Psalm 119:15). Such an alignment will result in the sanctification of the individual and the church (1 Thessalonians 5:23; 1 Corinthians 1:2; Hebrews 10:14; Ephesians 5:27). Sanctification, of course, requires right living, which only can be achieved if one first understands the difference between right and wrong, truth and error. As Jesus said, "You will know the truth, and the truth will set you free" (John 8:32). Even in his high priestly prayer, Jesus petitioned the Father that He would "sanctify [believers] in the truth; your word is truth" (John 17:17). In short, truth matters and it comes only from God.

Perhaps the best word to describe someone who understands the difference between godly and worldly thinking is the word "discerning." This characterizes the analytical thinking of a mature believer. Discernment is defined as the ability to judge well; it is the quality of being able to grasp and comprehend that which is obscure.[24]

---

23 As discussed later, this is not to say that believers can never learn from non-Christians, whether in the classroom or through on-the-job training. There are times when such subordinate learning is appropriate or necessary. However, this discussion centers on the biblical principles to consider when choosing a four-year college when more than one option is available.

24 *Merriam-Webster*, s.v. "Discernment," accessed October 5, 2015, http://www.merriam-webster.com/dictionary/discernment.

"Biblical discernment" is defined as "the ability to decide between truth and error, right and wrong. Discernment is the process of making careful distinctions in one's thinking about truth. In other words, the ability to think with discernment is synonymous with an ability to think biblically."[25]

To be clear, the Bible not only esteems discernment, but God commands it for His children. A discerning mind is the only way to properly evaluate moral issues. In 1 Thessalonians 5:21-22, believers are commanded to "test everything; hold fast what is good. Abstain from every form of evil." Paul, as he encouraged the Philippian believers in their spiritual walks, indicated that it was his "prayer that your love may abound more and more, with knowledge and all discernment, so that you may approve what is excellent, and so be pure and blameless for the day of Christ" (Philippians 1:9-10). Likewise, 1 John 4:1 states that believers should "not believe every spirit, but test the spirits to see whether they are from God, for many false prophets have gone out into the world." In other words, true followers of Christ are required to judge that which is from God (truth) and that which is not. Whatever is not of God should be avoided.

Becoming a discerning believer takes practice. In explaining that discernment comes from consistent spiritual practice and discipline, Paul advises that it is nearly impossible for immature believers to skillfully live righteous lives: "But solid food is for the mature, for those who have their powers of discernment trained by constant practice to distinguish good from evil" (Hebrews 5:14). Indeed, without discernment, Christians are at risk of remaining in a perpetual state of spiritual immaturity, "tossed to and fro by the waves and carried about by every wind of doctrine, by human cunning, by craftiness in deceitful schemes" (Ephesians 4:14). They will be unable to live an uncompromised life since they will be subject to all kinds of false teaching and they will not run to the infallible Scriptures that

---

25 John MacArthur, "What is Biblical Discernment and Why is it Important?" *Grace to You*, accessed January 19, 2015, http://www.gty.org/resources/questions/QA138/What-is-biblical-discernment-and-why-is-it-important.

provide all that is necessary for life and godliness (2 Peter 1:3).[26] Put another way, godly discernment from the Holy Spirit helps believers avoid sin since it is *the* mental mechanism that allows the individual to distinguish between right and wrong, good and bad, moral and immoral. Accordingly, if a college experience does not promote biblical discernment and if it instead results in stagnated (or negative) spiritual growth, it is not a four-year experience that God intends for His children.

College Should Involve the Pursuit of Wisdom

The goal of a college experience (and life) should be to glorify God.[27] As demonstrated above, this goal is advanced by basing education and activities on biblical principles and fostering discernment among believers, which will provide the tools necessary to live a wise life. Only a person wise in the things of God will live a life pleasing to God, which is why a college experience should encourage the pursuit of godly wisdom (Ecclesiastes 2:13).

Scripture touts the benefits of wisdom. Proverbs 16:16 says that it is "better to get wisdom than gold!" Upon reading this verse, the believer who claims to trust God and His Word is forced to decide whether to pursue the riches that the world has to offer or to pursue the wisdom that God offers. The path to that wisdom is well-marked: "The fear of the LORD is the beginning of wisdom, and the knowledge of the Holy One is insight" (Proverbs 9:10). The fear and knowledge of God are found by studying Scripture (2 Timothy 3:15, "the sacred writings, which are able to make you wise for salvation through faith in Christ Jesus"). Since this wisdom actually leads to eternal salvation, it makes absolutely no sense for a believer to spend time being "educated" in a system that may lead him away from God's Word. In fact, it is the fool who despises such wisdom (Proverbs 1:7).[28]

Knowing that education and the overall college experience should

---

26 MacArthur, "What is Biblical Discernment and Why is it Important?"

27 *See* Wilson, *Why Christian Kids Need a Christian Education*, 23.

28 Although there is a level of wisdom unbelievers can grasp through the study of nature or general revelation, the unbelieving mind is incapable of a comprehensive, correct under-standing—and certainly of God's involvement—without submission to God's Word.

be based on biblical principles, should foster biblical discernment, and should pursue godly wisdom, a four-year college journey should be designed to carry the student along the spiritual spectrum, ever increasing his ability to properly evaluate what is being offered to him by the world in light of Scripture, and to make wise choices—all while equipping him to contribute by living a responsible and excellent life.

CHAPTER 5

INFLUENCES AND PURSUITS

In three short verses at the beginning of the book of Psalms, God provides perfect insight into what people should pursue and why, and what (and whom) they should avoid. Following this advice leads to blessedness, happiness, fruitfulness, and satisfaction; not following it leads to cursedness, unhappiness, and judgment.[29] Those choosing a place to spend the next four years of their lives would do well to read, understand, and implement the counsel provided by the psalmist before making their final college selection.

> Blessed is the man
> who walks not in the counsel of the wicked,
> nor stands in the way of sinners,
> nor sits in the seat of scoffers;
> but his delight is in the law of the LORD,
> and on his law he meditates day and night.
>
> He is like a tree
> planted by streams of water
> that yields its fruit in its season,
> and its leaf does not wither.
> In all that he does, he prospers. (Psalm 1:1-3)

Up through medieval times, what is now known as Psalm 1 actually appeared in manuscripts without a chapter number or verses.[30] It was understood to be an introduction to the entire Psalter, as opposed to the first of many psalms. This introduction was written as both an exhortation and encouragement, and acted as a gateway to the wisdom that followed.[31]

---

29 J. Hampton Keathley III, "Psalm 1: Two Ways of Life—A Psalm of Wisdom," *Bible.org*, accessed March 16, 2015, https://bible.org/article/psalm-1-two-ways-life-psalm-wisdom.

30 Gerald Wilson, *Psalms*, The NIV Application Commentary (Grand Rapids, MI: Zondervan, 2002), 1:92.

31 Ibid., *Psalms*, 1:92.

Before delving into the analysis and application of Psalm 1, it must first be recognized that there are at least three different views about what the psalmist meant when he wrote about the wicked, the sinners, and the scoffers (v. 1). The first is that the warning is to avoid being *influenced* by the wicked person; the second contends that the warning is to avoid *being* the wicked person; and the third is a combination of the two—avoid being influenced by an ungodly person to the point where one begins to partake in the ungodly conduct.[32] The distinction is not minor. For example, if the instruction is to avoid *ever* being advised or taught by the ungodly, then it would seem that no believer should ever sit under the tutelage of a non-believer on any subject. Taken to an extreme, one can see how this reading would prevent Christian medical students from learning from unbelievers how to set broken bones, it would disallow Christian mechanics from learning from non-Christians how to change spark plugs, and it would virtually preclude any believer from taking instruction from a non-believing boss. This cannot be the correct reading since Scripture teaches in other contexts that there are times when believers are to submit to the authority and instruction of non-Christians, so long as the instruction is not contrary to God's law (Romans 13:1-7; 1 Peter 2:13-14; Acts 5:27-29). On the other hand, it also cannot be read to mean that being influenced by others to engage in ungodly behavior is acceptable since that, too, runs afoul of Scripture (Deuteronomy 13:6-8; Proverbs 1:10; 14:7).

The Hebrew definitions of the words employed by the psalmist are helpful. Some of them are inserted in parenthesis in this recitation of verse 1: "Blessed is the man who walks (behaves) not in the counsel (advice, scheme, and plan) of the wicked, nor stands (endures, perseveres) in the way (custom, behavior, path) of sinners, nor sits (remains, dwells) in the seat (position, habitation, residence)

---

32 *See, e.g.,* H. D. M. Spence-Jones, ed., *Psalms, vol. 1, The Pulpit Commentary* (London: Funk & Wagnalls Company, 1909), 1; Matthew Henry, *Matthew Henry's Commentary on the Whole Bible: Complete and Unabridged in One Volume* (Peabody, MA: Hendrickson Publishing, 1994), 743; Robert Jamieson, A. R. Fausset, and David Brown, *Commentary Critical and Explanatory on the Whole Bible*, vol. 1 (Oak Harbor, WA: Logos Research Systems, Inc., 1997), 346; Allen P. Ross, "Psalms," in *The Bible Knowledge Commentary: An Exposition of the Scriptures*, ed. J. F. Walvoord and R. B. Zuck, vol. 1 (Wheaton, IL: Victor Books, 1985), 790.

of scoffers."[33] From this reading, it appears that the instruction is to avoid *participating* in the scorn of evildoers. It also does not negate the implicit instruction to avoid the undue influence of the ungodly, which can lead to ungodliness. As one commentator put it, this verse "signifies a progression from a casual influence of ungodly people to collusion with them in their scorn against the righteous. One who is *not* characterized by this evil influence is 'blessed,' that is, he is right with God and enjoys the spiritual peace and joy that results from that relationship."[34]

With the above in mind, it appears that there are two primary points of emphasis. First, God affirms blessings on those who avoid certain behaviors and certain influential associations. Second, God explains the proper focus of a man's life (God's Word) and the sure footing that it provides. Indeed, anyone looking for a concise and precise explanation of how to succeed in God's eyes will find it in this passage.

To begin with, the psalmist provides an example of a life *not* to be copied, which by implication, seems to indicate that one cannot easily apply his mind to God's Word without first separating himself from overly influential, ungodly associations.[35] This is consistent with the New Testament teaching that believers are not to be unequally bound in partnership (yoked) with non-believers; after all, "what partnership has righteousness with lawlessness? Or what fellowship has light with darkness?" (2 Corinthians 6:14). In fact, the warning in Psalm 1 follows the progression of an individual who descends into wickedness. Blessings are promised to the one who does *not* follow this progression. Whether one interprets verse 1 to warn against *being* a wicked scorner, or whether it warns against *being influenced* by such a person to the point where the student takes on the same evil characteristics, the results are the same—separation from God's blessings. The verbs used in this progression (walk, stand, sit) provide an illustration that every reader can understand.

---

33 *See generally* Chip McDaniel, *The English-Hebrew Reverse Interlinear Old Testament English Standard Version*, Lexham Press, 2009.

34 Ross, "Psalms," in *The Bible Knowledge Commentary: An Exposition of the Scriptures*, 790.

35 John Calvin, *Commentary on the Book of Psalms*, trans. James Anderson (Grand Rapids, MI: Wm. B. Eerdmans Publishing Company, 1948), 2.

For example, someone destined to be influenced for evil first "walks" alongside a wicked person, then stops ("stands") to spend more time with him,[36] and then ultimately takes up "permanent residence" ("sits") in his company.[37] In short, when a person associates with and lives in sin and with sinners, he typically goes from bad to worse (1 Corinthians 15:33).[38] Then, of course, he himself becomes the wicked person who casts scorn on believers and who influences others to do the same (Psalm 1:1).

As to the types of people who are *not* blessed, the psalmist identifies three. The first, the "wicked," denotes someone who has been adjudged as guilty in a court of law.[39] This person does not live up to God's standards; he is godless and his morals are lax.[40] He is ungodly, even if carelessly so.[41] The second, the "sinner," calls to mind someone who has not simply committed an isolated or careless, sinful act, but one whose inclinations are to sin and whose life makes a career out of sinning,[42] especially coarse and manifest sin.[43] The final person, the "scoffer" (or "mocker"), is one whose life is not only dominated by sin, but who takes affirmative steps to mock or express disdain for those who pursue and advocate righteousness.[44] This person directs his jesting to that which is holy, noble, and true.[45] He is a pestilent teacher and tempter of others.[46] He claims to be master over his own path (Psalm 12:4). In his mocking, he confidently ridicules those who wait for God's deliverance, since (according to the mocker) God will never actually respond (Psalm 10:6, 11). This foolish scoffer says,

---

36 The Hebrew word used for "stand" in this context can also be translated "take a stand," which implies an affirmative act as opposed to a passive acquiescence. Wilson, *Psalms*, 1:94n15.

37 Ibid., 94.

38 Charles Spurgeon, "The Treasury of David: Psalm 1," *The Spurgeon Archive*, accessed March 13, 2015, http://www.spurgeon.org/treasury/ps001.htm.

39 Wilson, *Psalms*, 1:94.

40 Franz Delitzsch, *Biblical Commentary on the Psalms* (Edinburgh: Morrison and Gibb, 1892), 84.

41 Spurgeon, "The Treasury of David: Psalm 1."

42 Wilson, *Psalms*, 1:95.

43 Delitzsch, *Biblical Commentary on the Psalm*, 84.

44 Wilson, *Psalms*, 1:95.

45 Delitzsch, *Biblical Commentary on the Psalms*, 84.

46 Spurgeon, "The Treasury of David: Psalm 1."

"There is no God" (Psalm 14:1). He is an abomination to mankind (Proverbs 24:9).

Although Psalm 1:1 clearly condemns the wicked, scoffing sinner, his influence is also condemned (consistent with 1 Corinthians 15:33 and Proverbs 13:20) to the point where a reasonable warning may sound like this in modern language: *Do not pass through the overly influential company of an ungodly person who commits intentional or careless sin with no regard to God (or the gratification of the sin will infatuate you);[47] do not intentionally spend significant time with an influential person whose life is marked by intentional and habituated sin (or you will become hardened in your wickedness); and do not learn from, hitch your life to, or provide support for a person who makes it his practice to mock righteous living (or you will become stubborn and start to participate not only in this practice, but also in luring others away from righteous living).[48]* Even a person who has not yet been totally defiled by this sin may start to resemble the wicked by imitating their corrupt manners and lifestyles.[49] In fact, this passage also can be applied to one who initially hears out a sinner in his folly, who then voluntarily spends time in the influential presence of and learns from a habitual sinner, and who then so buys into that belief system and lifestyle that he is permanently associated with such an anti-God viewpoint that he "sits" in a place of godless authority to pass those godless beliefs on to others. After all, one's "example is not the main thing in influencing others. It is the only thing."[50]

The dangers warned against in Psalm 1:1 stand in stark contrast to the commands given to God's children in Deuteronomy 6:4-9. In that passage, the Israelites were commanded to teach God's commands to

---

47 *See* T.M. Moore, "Ease and Indulgence," *The Chuck Colson Center for Christian Worldview*, accessed April 21, 2015, http://www.colsoncenter.org/the-center/columns/worldview-bible/22817-ease-and-indulgence ("One way we can know that we're being confronted by temptation is when we find ourselves admiring wickedness, seeing only what appeals to us and none of the dangers, and beginning to imagine ourselves getting in on some of that action.").

48 Calvin, *Commentary on the Book of Psalms*, 3.

49 Ibid., 4.

50 Albert Schweitzer, *Albert Schweitzer: Thoughts for Our Times,*" ed. Erica Anderson (Mount Vernon, NY: The Peter Pauper Press, 1975).

their family members at all times ("when you sit in your house, and when you walk by the way, and when you lie down, and when you rise"). The idea is a total immersion into God's commands, to the point where they permeate one's entire life.[51] There is a seriousness to the study of God's Word and, consistent with Psalm 1:2-3, this total surrender and gobbling up of God's Word leads to blessings, steadfastness, and a firm foundation.

The application of the above passage to the issue of "where and with whom" believers should spend their time is clear:

- Avoid the influence of those who intentionally sin (1 Corinthians 5:11; Proverbs 4:14-15).

- Do not voluntarily spend time with them where sinful habits will rub off (1 Corinthians 15:33; Proverbs 13:20), and certainly do not give in to the point where you are providing support and even teaching others a disdain for God's Word (Colossians 2:8; Psalm 26:4-5). Instead, turn away from them (Romans 16:17; Galatians 1:6-9; Proverbs 14:7), unless the goal is good works and sharing the gospel (Matthew 28:16-20; Galatians 6:10; Acts 1:8).[52]

- Seek to be a companion to those who fear God and obey Him (Psalm 119:63). This is the law of life: One either aggressively pursues his relationship with God through His Word, or he sins more and more and more, until he is engaged in active rebellion against God (*see* Hebrews 3:13; the deceitfulness of sin hardens hearts). Remaining passive and neutral is not an option.[53]

---

51 Wilson, *Psalms*, 1:94.

52 Nothing herein should be interpreted as discouraging kind and respectful interactions with non-believers for the purpose of sharing the good news. In fact, Christians should always be prepared to give an answer for the hope that lies within them (1 Peter 3:15). However, when Christians cease to be influencers, it is time to depart (Matthew 10:14). In this passage, the psalmist is simply warning against adopting the attitude and lifestyle of the wicked, which typically starts by spending inordinate amounts of time with those whose attitudes rebel against submission to the Creator.

53 Keathley III, "Psalm 1: Two Ways of Life—A Psalm of Wisdom."

Psalm 1:1 and 1 Corinthians 15:33 ("bad company ruins good morals") apply to a wide variety of real-life, 21st century situations. Not only do these passages have direct application to friendships, partnerships, and acquaintances, but much can be said of the time spent under the influence of the wickedness found on television, movies, video games, magazines, books, music, and the Internet. Put another way, how much time are we spending with God's Word when compared to these worldly influences? Have we passed through their presence? Have they caught our eyes and tempted us? Have we spent significant time under their influence? Have our lives been habituated and hardened to their presence in our lives, to the point where we are not nearly as shocked or disturbed by them as we were initially? Do our lives look like we celebrate, enjoy, and support their messages? In short, has this wickedness brought us to the point of learning and being influenced by sinners who have no regard for things of God? Are we wicked, sinful scorners? And, perhaps most important, have we gotten to the point where we are passing sinful attitudes, comments, and habits on to others? If so, we may have been unequally yoked with unbelievers (2 Corinthians 6:14) and their sin is now our sin.[54]

Applying this thinking to the college selection process, the following questions should be asked by believers:

> 1. Will attending this college put me in a position where I will be in constant contact with those who intentionally and unrepentantly sin? What type of people will I be mostly in contact with? Do they pursue righteousness or ungodliness? Will I be influenced to behave the way they do? Who will I be studying with? Who will I live with? Who will be in my classes? If the positions I hold begin to resemble theirs, will I be closer to or further from God?

---

54 While Paul's command to not be unequally yoked with non-believers applies to spiritual enterprises, care should be taken not to think that only religious-sounding experiences constitute such spiritual enterprises. For example, marriage is a spiritual enterprise, just as much as a religious ceremony. The same may be said for certain business and other intimate relationships, including friendships and, possibly, teacher-student relations, *depending on the context*. Not all such relationships require Christians to withdraw; but if spiritual influence and ministry are contemplated in such settings, believers and non-believers have no unity of interest. *See generally* John MacArthur, "Separating from Unbelievers, Part I," Sermon, Grace Community Church, July 23, 1995.

2. Will attending this college lead me to sit at the feet of scoffers (unholy teachers) and, ultimately, associate me with such persons to the point where others look to me as if I am endorsing their beliefs? Will I become a scoffer by attending? Who will be teaching me? Do the professors love God and His Word, or not? Do they affirmatively advance non-Christian teaching or celebrate sinful lifestyles and beliefs? Do they mock those who rely on Scripture as a guide for daily living? As part of my coursework, will I be required to advance such ideas or, at a minimum, will I be tempted to remain silent to protect my grades?

3. How spiritually mature am I? (This is a question that must be answered by Scripture and in consultation with more mature believers.) Do I think I am beyond the influence of evil and, if not, is there *any* risk that my mind will slowly be turned against God's clear commands? And, if I believe I am immune to the influence of evil, have I already lost my way by ignoring 1 Corinthians 10:12 and 15:33 and do I need to repent and seriously make sure that the college I choose will not lead me into further temptation?[55]

If there is any doubt as to where the best return on investment will come from, it is found in verses 2 and 3. God promises that the one who avoids undue wicked influence and, instead, delights in His Word, will be like a strong tree that yields fruit at the exact right time (Psalm 1:2-3; *see also* Psalm 11:7, "For the LORD is righteous; he loves righteous deeds; the upright shall behold His face"; Isaiah 66:2, "But this is the one to whom I will look: he who is humble and contrite in spirit and trembles at my word"). This is the opposite of the

---

55 To the extent a student thinks himself immune to the influence of professors, studies have shown that despite their desire to "be free" from adult influence, students tend to reflect the values of their professors even 25 years later. *See* Steve Henderson, "Investing in Their Faith," accessed April 16, 2015, *Christian College Guide*, http://www.christian-collegeguide.net/article/Investing-in-Their-Faith?page=2. This is true despite the fact that nearly two-thirds of college students say that their professors never encourage discussions of spiritual/religious matters. Alexander Astin and Helen Astin, "Spirituality in Higher Education: Study Reveals Influences of College on Students' Spiritual and Religious Development," *Spirituality.UCLA.edu*, Higher Education Research Institute, accessed January 30, 2016, http://spirituality.ucla.edu/docs/news/release_college_experience.pdf.

scoffer. So, to the extent that any college seems appealing based on the benefits that come with such an education, consideration should first be given to whether attending such a school will advance or hinder the student's consistent meditation on God's Word. After all, college is a place where the entire point *is to be influenced.* In other words, the wise Christian student and parent will ally themselves with God as opposed to exalting human reputation and wisdom. Unlike the sturdy and watered tree, the wicked will not endure, nor will their teaching (Psalm 1:4). They will *not* stand in the congregation of the righteous (Psalm 1:5). They will never enter the kingdom of heaven (Matthew 7:21; 1 Corinthians 6:9; John 3:5).[56] And the one who does not avoid becoming tainted by their evil influence will meet the same destruction.[57]

---

56 Jesus gave clear warning to those who mislead others. "Temptations to sin are sure to come, but woe to the one through whom they come! It would be better for him if a millstone were hung around his neck and he were cast into the sea than that he should cause one of these little ones to sin" (Luke 17:1-2; *see also* Psalm 2:1-5).

57 Calvin, *Commentary on the Book of Psalms*, 3. In his commentary on this Psalm, John Calvin warns against being carried away by the ungodliness of others (which he says Christians should abhor) since it leads away—little by little—from God's righteous path.

CHAPTER 6

GOD DEFINES SUCCESS
AND GUARANTEES RESULTS

IS YOUR DEFINITION OF SUCCESS
THE SAME AS GOD'S DEFINITION?

Most people considering college are trying to figure out which institution will pave the path to the most successful life. Some characterize success as money, others characterize it as prestige, some seek to learn and increase their intelligence or skill, while others seek positions of power.[58] However, since a believer should be doing everything for the glory of God (1 Corinthians 10:31) and should seek to know God's will (Deuteronomy 4:29; Proverbs 8:17; Lamentations 3:25), perhaps one pertinent question to be asked is this: How does God define success? After all, He designed humans and He alone holds the keys to eternal life (John 14:6). I don't know about you, but I want *Him* to call my life a success.

To begin with, godly success involves knowing and doing God's will. After Moses died, leadership of God's people was passed to Joshua. The Lord's words to Joshua are instructive to anyone seeking the favor of the Lord:

> This Book of the Law shall not depart from your mouth,
> but you shall meditate on it day and night, so that you

---

58 With the ever-increasing rise of materialism in the western world, the goal of "being very well off financially" has grown dramatically in college students, while the goal of "developing a meaningful philosophy of life" has declined sharply. Alexander Astin, Helen Astin, Jennifer Lindholm, *Cultivating the Spirit: How College Can Enhance Students' Inner Lives* (San Francisco, CA: John Wiley & Sons, Inc., 2011), 2. As one popular college preparation website states, a college education should be designed to "unlock opportunities" in order to "get a job; keep a job; make more money." Big Future, "College: What It's All About and Why it Matters," *College Board*, accessed January 30, 2016, https://bigfuture. collegeboard.org/get-started/know-yourself/college-what-its-all-about-and-why-it-matters.

may be careful to do according to all that is written in it. For then you will make your way prosperous, and then you will have good success. Have I not commanded you? Be strong and courageous. Do not be frightened, and do not be dismayed, for the LORD your God is with you wherever you go. (Joshua 1:8-9)

The passage is clear. In order to achieve success in the Lord's eyes, Joshua was to study God's Word and obey it. Further, the Lord did not leave Joshua alone in this endeavor. He promised to be with him on this journey to success. Indeed, no one can navigate such a journey— or even begin it—without God's divine involvement (John 4:23; Romans 3:10-11).

So as not to leave people wondering whether the success that God values involves worldly possessions, strength, or intelligence, He provided the following contrast.

Let not the wise man boast in his wisdom, let not the mighty man boast in his might, let not the rich man boast in his riches, but let him who boasts boast in this, that he understands and knows me, that I am the Lord who practices steadfast love, justice, and righteousness in the earth. For in these things I delight, declares the Lord. (Jeremiah 9:23-24)

There you have it. Success in God's eyes is not measured the way the world measures success. Instead, it is knowing God through His Word, understanding Him, and obeying Him. Is that the kind of success you had in mind when you initially were considering college choices?

Do You Need the Big School Name on Your Résumé for God to Accomplish Great Things Through You?

"But I need to attend a good secular college so that I can get into graduate school or get a good job. No one will take me seriously if I attend a Christian school. They'll just think I studied the Bible all the time and didn't learn anything useful!" Although those exact words may not have crossed your lips, perhaps those thoughts have crossed your mind. The truth is, the world does *not* view Christian schools the same as secular institutions.[59]

More specifically, although many Christian colleges offer world class educations, it is unrealistic to suggest that degrees from many Christian schools carry the same *worldly* weight as those from institutions that enjoy high rankings in the world's eyes. In more blunt terms, a believer who opts to forego a secular education *might* very well be giving up certain future opportunities in this lifetime in exchange for a serious Christian education. Why? The world, through its own wisdom, *cannot* find or know God (1 Corinthians 2:14); this deficiency, however, does not stop it from puffing up to the point of dictating how all people must think. This worldly perspective looks down on graduates who have not studied with the "approved people" at the "approved institutions."[60] The world does not reason; it shames. However, such a response should not dissuade a believer from attending a college where light is taught if that is where God leads. After all, God's Word is a lamp and a light (Psalm 119:105), and because of that illumination, God's children "have more understanding than all my teachers, for your testimonies are my meditation. I understand more than the aged, for I keep your precepts" (Psalm 119:99-100). Likewise, "God chose what is foolish in the world to shame the wise; God chose what is weak in the world to shame the strong" (1 Corinthians 1:27). Do you trust that God can and will place you where He wants you to be (graduate school, job, position), even without that supposedly prestigious diploma on your résumé? Or must you have that diploma to pursue all that *you* desire in life? To the extent that making a decision to pursue a Christ-centered education results in a believer needing to rely even more on God, it should be remembered with affection that Christ's power is made perfect in the weakness of those who call him Lord (2 Corinthians

---

59 Unfortunately, too many parents and students associate Christian colleges with training only pastors or Bible teachers. Such an understanding does an injustice to the sophisticated and well-rounded education that many Christian colleges offer, and is grounded in an inaccurate view of education that likely has been formed by pooled ignorance disseminated over the course of decades of anti-Christian thought.

60 Douglas Wilson, "Biologs, Respectability, and Classical Christian Education," *Blog and Mablog*, accessed May 27, 2015, http://dougwils.com/s7-engaging-the-culture/biologos-respectability-and-classical-christian-education.html.

12:9). Is the Lord your "strength" and "shield"? (Psalm 28:7). Or are you relying on something else when choosing a college?[61]

Are You Pursuing the Right Things?

> It would seem that Our Lord finds our desires not too strong, but too weak. We are half-hearted creatures, fooling about with drink and sex and ambition when infinite joy is offered us, like an ignorant child who wants to go on making mud pies in a slum because he cannot imagine what is meant by the offer of a holiday at the sea. We are far too easily pleased.[62]

When C.S. Lewis penned these words, he was perhaps not thinking about choosing a college. He was presenting the Christian belief in a forceful and accessible way, and he certainly was thinking about the fact that humans are easily lured and consumed by filth and rubbish (which can include the pursuit of worldly success), even to the point of ignoring the wonderful things that God has in store for them. In the same work, Lewis wrote that, "He who has God and everything else has no more than he who has God only."[63] The idea is that humans tend to pursue that which the world offers *as if it were better or more important than (or could somehow improve) that which God already has promised!* In simple terms, when believers strive after worldly success, recognition, or riches, they are missing the point that God has so clearly explained in His Word. Scripture provides the best summary of this point:

---

61 This author is not convinced that attending a Christian college will erect barriers to those whom God has gifted and to those who work hard. The world is in need and still hires motivated, hard-working individuals who strive for excellence, whether they find cures for diseases or whether they can weld perfect joints on construction projects. However, even if a sacrifice were required to attend a Christian college in order to better know the almighty, loving God and His commandments, isn't that exactly what the Bible calls for believers to do? (*See* Matthew 16:24). As the last line goes in the hymn, When I Survey The Wondrous Cross: "Love so amazing, so divine, demands my soul, my life, my all." Isaac Watts, "When I Survey The Wondrous Cross, Timeless Truths, accessed October 5, 2015, http://library.timelesstruths.org/music/When_I_Survey_the_Wondrous_Cross/ (public domain, 1707).

62 C.S. Lewis, *The Weight of Glory* (New York: The MacMillan Company, 1949), 1-2.

63 Ibid., *The Weight of Glory*, 7.

Come, everyone who thirsts, come to the waters;
And he who has no money, come, buy and eat!
Come, buy wine and milk without money and without price.
Why do you spend your money for that which is not bread,
And your labor for that which does not satisfy?
Listen diligently to me, and eat what is good,
And delight yourselves in rich food.
Incline your ear, and come to me;
Hear, that your soul may live. (Isaiah 55:1-3)

In very simple terms, God offers all that satisfies, including eternal life—for free! Jesus made the same guarantee during his Sermon on the Mount when he promised the earth, righteousness, mercy, the entire kingdom of heaven, and even God Himself to those who hold fast to God's promises and who thirst for and follow Him (Matthew 5). In short, nothing good will be withheld from God's children; everything will work together for the good of those who love Him and who are called according to His purpose (Romans 8:28).

When put into the college selection context, certain questions arise. Why are we striving so hard to achieve something that God already has promised? Why do we think we will not be satisfied with an education that is based on God's Word? Why do we think we must immerse ourselves in the world's education system when it may require subjecting ourselves to the significant influence of anti-Christian sentiment and values?

First, many of God's children do not trust God and His promises. While most Christians say they trust God, and they say they believe His promises, they tend to speak with big picture, eternal, Christian-sounding vocabulary. Their "trust" has no real impact on their daily lives. They do not understand or believe that eternal life began when God saved them. They do not lay hold of the guarantee that His children are redeemed through the blood of Christ, they are forgiven, and they are full heirs to the inheritance of His grace (Ephesians 1:7). In terms of college choice, they do not recognize that a degree from the highest ranking school, securing the highest paying job, or achieving the most powerful title in the company will not provide perfect satisfaction. Only God can provide such peace. His children would do well to seek God first and trust Him completely for all things (Matthew 6:33; Proverbs 3:5-6).

Second, there are those (even in the church) who pursue results instead of pursuing God. Not convinced? Look at the charismatic movement. Many people are overwhelmingly pursuing the "experience" of the Holy Spirit as they perceive it. They want the "feeling" that they think should come from His presence. However, instead of pursuing a feeling—which results in a counterfeit and temporary satisfaction—they should pursue God Himself who promises a lasting peace that surpasses all comprehension (Philippians 4:7). The same can be said at the other end of the spectrum. Many fundamentalists strive to follow a strict set of rules, as if obedience is the actual prize to be obtained. However, if they simply were to pursue God, their lives would transform and obedience would follow (Romans 12:2; Galatians 5:22-23). How about the health and wealth movement? People are called to give more generously and to have more faith *so that* they can receive health and/or the material benefits that this world offers. As the title of one such book teaches, you can have "Your Best Life Now."[64]

Unfortunately, all who follow this misguided counsel are missing out not only on eternal life, but also on the benefits that God offers to those who pursue Him. These individuals are not seeking the Master; they are seeking what they perceive is sitting on the Master's table. Judas Iscariot fell into this category. He was part of a select group of men who spent significant time with Jesus, but he did not love Jesus. He simply loved what he thought he could get out of Jesus. He enjoyed the superficial benefits of being associated with Jesus and did not pursue God. The same can be said of the crowds who ushered Jesus into Jerusalem and who were rejoicing and praising God "for all the mighty works that they had seen" (Luke 19:37). But these same crowds were clamoring for his crucifixion just days later when it became apparent that he had no intention to overthrow the government that Rome had set up in their city (Matthew 27:22-23). Again, they were focusing on miraculous deeds and their personal

---

64 Joel Osteen, *Your Best Life Now* (New York: FaithWords, 2004).

desires as opposed to eternal life and Jesus' call to repentance. In doing so, they missed out on the satisfying and joyous gift that Jesus came to give.[65]

Now take a fresh look at C.S. Lewis's previous quotes. He had it right. People spend a great deal of time, money, and energy pursuing things or accomplishments that add no lasting value to their lives, and that certainly have no value in eternity. They simply do not understand or appreciate all that He offers. In the hymn, *Praise to the Lord, The Almighty,* one line goes like this: "Hast thou not seen how all thy desires have been granted in what He ordaineth?"[66] God's children do not need to exhaust themselves chasing their dreams of a good degree, a well-paying job, a nice house, or the perfect spouse. Although there is nothing wrong with any of these, and God can and does grant them to His children in varying degrees, the problem arises when people start such pursuits thinking that, "*If only* I get X, then I will be happy or satisfied." That is a lie from the pit of hell (or the heart of man). Achieving worldly success or pleasure does *not* satisfy. It merely provides an unstable stepping stone to the next worldly pursuit. When multimillionaire John D. Rockefeller was asked, "How much money is enough?" he responded, "Just a little bit more."[67] As one author so elegantly stated,

> Visible results can be deceptive. In the seen world, we may appear to make a great advance—win professional recognition, attract people to our cause, raise money for our program, distribute tons of literature, win passage of an important bill. But if it was done by humanistic reliance on technical methods, without

---

65 This concept of people pursuing results instead of God was planted in my mind through a number of sermons and talks given by my pastor and friend, Steve Balentine, over the course of a few years at San Gabriel Community Church in San Gabriel, California, during the time period from approximately 2013-2015.

66 Joachim Neander, "Praise to the Lord, the Almighty," *Timeless Truths*, accessed October 5, 2015, http://library.timelesstruths.org/music/Praise_to_the_Lord_the_Almighty/ (public domain, 1680).

67 *New World Encyclopedia*, s.v. "John D. Rockefeller," accessed May 27, 2016, http://www.newworldencyclopedia.org/entry/John_D._Rockefeller; E.G. Link, "How Much is Enough?" *Stewardship Ministries*, accessed April 8, 2015, http://www.stewardshipministries.org/blog/2012/03/01/how-much-is-enough/.

the leading of the Spirit, then we have accomplished little of value in the unseen world. The opposite is likewise true: If Christians use the weapons God has ordained—if we lay our talents at His feet, dying to our own pride and ambition, obeying biblical moral principles, empowered by His Spirit, guided by a Christian worldview perspective—then even if by external standards we seem to have lost, *we really have won* ... When life ends and we stand at the believers' judgment described in 1 Corinthians 3, some of our most successful and impressive projects may prove to be nothing but wood, hay, and stubble—devoured by the flames. But the activities that were truly led and empowered by God, in obedience to His truth, whether the results were visible or not, will sparkle as gold, silver, and precious stones. And God will set them as jewels in our heavenly crown.[68]

If the goal in choosing a college is propelled by the desire for worldly pleasure, personal success, or wealth, then the focus is wrong (*see* Jeremiah 45:5). Believers should not strive to gain things that God already has made freely available to His children, who are heirs to the riches of His grace (Ephesians 1:7). During the college selection process, believers should take care to not lose focus as they prioritize the reasons for their education and their love for God. He has already guaranteed perfect peace and joy to those who follow Him. Do you trust Him enough to trust Him with your choice of a college?

> Turn your eyes upon Jesus,
> Look full in His wonderful face,
> And the things of earth will grow strangely dim,
> In the light of His glory and grace.[69]

---

68 Pearcey, *Total Truth*, 363-64.

69 Helen Lemmel, "Turn Your Eyes Upon Jesus," *Timeless Truths*, accessed October 5, 2015, http://library.timelesstruths.org/music/Turn_Your_Eyes_upon_Jesus/ (public domain, 1922).

CHAPTER 7

IS THERE REALLY IS A DIFFERENCE AND DOES IT MATTER?

There are those who will read all of the above, yet still wonder whether a Christian college is a significantly better choice than a secular college. Some may either be too caught up in what they perceive to be a better academic experience, or they will be enticed by the worldly prestige and success that they anticipate a secular degree at a highly ranked institution will offer.[70] As to the first point, do not be deceived. While there are many secular institutions that provide quality skill training, facilities, and professors, even the best secular education provides an incomplete education. It is not based on God, and "God is light" (1 John 1:5). To a certain extent, a secular education is akin to studying in the dark and, as one author put it, "Studying in the dark is not objective; it is stupid."[71] While it may be argued that all human institutions (even Christian ones) provide an incomplete understanding of God and cannot perfectly integrate Scripture with all subjects, the question is whether or not one choice is a markedly better school for a Christian to attend when compared with others that make no attempt to incorporate Christian thought into the curriculum. To this question, it must be admitted that more light is better than no light (*see* Matthew 13:12; Proverbs 13:20). However, do not be deceived. The greatest enemy to a college student is *not* dark input from a secular education. Instead, it is the negative influence of self-centeredness, godless thinking, and gospel ignorance, each of which can be present in every student's life at any institution. However, by God's grace and blessing and the application of Scripture, the prayer is that these traits are affirmatively designated as enemy combatants

---

70 As set forth elsewhere in this book, this is not intended to paint every decision to attend a secular college as an ungodly or wrong choice. There are legitimate reasons for doing so, but not every decision to attend such a college is based on those limited reasons.

71 *See* Wilson, *Why Christian Kids Need a Christian Education*, 37.

and are the focus of daily battles on an institutional basis at Christian colleges, where truth and light are taught.

As to the second point—again—do not be deceived. Prestige and success in the world are not all that they promise to be. "For what will it profit a man if he gains the whole world and forfeits his soul? Or what shall a man give in return for his soul?" (Matthew 16:26). While attending a secular college does not, by itself, damn a student to hell, studying and pursuing what the world offers can lead away from God. In other words, just like a mobile phone battery is in a constant state of dying when unplugged, it is the same for a believer who is "unplugged" from consistent Christian fellowship, solid biblical study and teaching, and disciplined communion with the Holy Spirit. These are not easy to find at a secular college and, in fact, the world will seek to lead a student *away* from those things and toward the empty promise of worldly achievement and pleasure.[72] This is why the *overall* college experience should be considered in advance of making a school choice. That experience will be instrumental in developing a student's life and thinking during the college years.

As believing parents and students weigh the differences between a secular and Christian college, they should consider at least the following issues—whether the curriculum is stable, whether students are encouraged to discover truth, and whether the college promotes purity. The flip side of these issues is whether the student will be unduly influenced by wavering standards, whether the school discourages the pursuit of truth, and whether the school celebrates immorality.[73]

Does the School Provide Stable or Unstable Teaching?

A place of education should be stable, not wavering in beliefs, morals, curriculum, and goals. Being "double-minded" is not a compliment

---

72 As discussed elsewhere, Christian students in all schools should be involved in their local churches as well as other purposefully Christian organizations and activities (including the spiritual disciplines) to assist in their spiritual walks and lives of service.

73 Nothing herein should be construed to imply that there are no Christian professors at secular schools, or that some measure of truth is never taught in some of those institutions. The problem is that the ability to teach truth at secular schools is often restricted and, in many cases, absent.

(James 1:8). In that regard, modern, secular education is always changing, trying to be "progressive." This mindset implies a desire to "step out of the rut of history," which is a phrase expressing "a deep scorn for the past, a zeal for newness and rupture, an arrogance about old struggles and old accomplishments, a hastiness with inherited precedents and circumstances, a superstition about the magical powers of the present. It expresses also a generational view of history, which, like the view of history in terms of decades and centuries, is one of the shallowest views of all."[74] An unstable college ignores God's commandments and teachings that were set down long ago and refuses to acknowledge that God and His Word do not change (Malachi 3:6; Matthew 24:35).[75] Much of this teaching is based on "the shifting sand of 'what everybody knows' and 'the way we think today.'"[76]

Even setting aside questions of morality, there has been a marked change in modern-day curriculum from days past when a classical Christian education was presupposed in every American school. Students are no longer required to learn the basics that formed the foundation of an old liberal arts education where they were required to ask (and answer) the big questions in life such as, "Why are we here and where are we going?" Instead, students are encouraged to work collaboratively to reach consensus, esteem diversity in all areas of life, and accept almost any viewpoint, so long as it is not Christian. So even if the draw of a Bible-based education is not enough to pull you to a Christian college, perhaps the dumbing down of the typical western curriculum will cause you to re-think investing four years into the world's new system.[77]

---

74 Leon Wiesletier, "The Iran Deal and the Rut of History," *The Atlantic*, accessed July 27, 2015, http://www.theatlantic.com/international/archive/2015/07/iran-deal-history/399644/.

75 "One who marries the science of the day today should be prepared to be a widow tomorrow." Wilson, *Why Christian Kids Need a Christian Education*, 40. This means that things the world thinks are correct tend to be disproven later; but the Bible never changes. *See also* Conor Cunningham, "Theology Must Save Science From Naturalism," May 22, 2012, *Religion and Ethics*, accessed October 31, 2014, http://www.abc.net.au/religion/articles/2012/05/22/3508607.htm.

76 Phillip Johnson, foreword to *Total Truth*, by Nancy Pearcey, 13; *see also* Pearcey, *Total Truth*, 302 ("The idea that a single generation can reject wholesale all of Christian history and start over again is doomed to theological shallowness").

77 *See generally* Douglas Wilson, "Push Function Quit," *Blog and Mablog*, accessed May 27, 2015, http://dougwils.com/s7-engaging-the-culture/push-function-quit.html; *see also* Victor Davis Hanson, "The Regrettable Decline of Higher Learning," *National Review*,

Does the School Encourage Students to Discover Truth?

In the past, theology was always considered the "queen of the sciences." No matter how far scientists studied or dug into astronomy, mathematics, music, or logic, they always started and arrived at the same place—God. In other words, the Bible was considered the overarching standard of all truth, and the consistent and predictable laws of nature, physics, and mathematics could not be explained without the logical conclusion that an intelligent Creator was behind it all. From the beginning, God has invited man to subdue the earth (a task requiring much understanding) and to use reason (Genesis 1:26-28; Isaiah 1:18; Proverbs 27:17). Simply put, God is not afraid that the use of reason will lead away from Him. To the contrary, truth always leads to God.

Unfortunately, however, the world has exchanged the truth of God for a lie (Romans 1:25).[78] As one anti-Christian author put it when asked whether God's Word can be relied upon today, "There is not one major theological seminary, nor one Department of Religion in any major university, that teaches that nonsense."[79] Mankind has been given over to darkness and is blind to truth (Isaiah 44:18; 1 Corinthians 2:14; 2 Corinthians 4:4). A secular education, for example, teaches students to try to make sense of the world without ever referring to or acknowledging the existence of God.[80] Theology—the study of God—has now been supplanted at the top of the truth mountain by farcical and fantastical stories about how the world was created, yet none of these efforts provides a satisfactory explanation as to how this complex and amazing universe full of diverse creatures and things ever came into existence without an intelligent Creator. In fact, every

---

accessed February 6, 2016, http://www.nationalreview.com/article/430739/college-campus-safe-spaces-speech-codes-decline. Also, teachers have great influence on their students. In fact, "a disciple is not above his teacher, but everyone when he is fully trained will be like his teacher" (Luke 6:40). Therefore, responsible parents will care who is teaching—and influencing—their children.

78 This actually started in the Garden of Eden, when Eve listened to Satan's lies about what God had said (Genesis 3).

79 William Edelen, "The Bible and the Gullible," *Infidels.org*, accessed January 28, 2016, http://infidels.org/kiosk/article/the-bible-and-the-gullible-703.html.

80 Pearcey, *Total Truth*, 67.

explanation provided by the world not only leaves unanswered the main question (who started it all or put it here in the first place?), but at the same time, it contradicts another natural law (that of the "second law of thermodynamics") that says that everything declines into disorder or chaos, as opposed to evolving into orderly life forms and higher thinking. Even more puzzling is the world's new mantra that truth is relative. Apparently, it can change from person to person. Perhaps the dictionary definition of truth will need to be changed from that which is "in accordance with fact or reality,"[81] to "that which one decides to believe, whether based in reality or not."

On college campuses, we are now living in an age of enforced stupidity. Political correctness discourages people from discussing both sides of issues. In fact, the elite academia often demands that students adopt certain positions, while ridiculing those who question the premises of those positions. God, however, never says that humans should ignore facts. He wants people to reason with Him (Isaiah 1:18) and He declares, "Woe to those who call evil good and good evil" (Isaiah 5:20). But if a believer knows the truth, can't he just go along with the gag just to get passing grades, secure a degree, and graduate? No. Believers confront error and pursue truth because God is truth (John 14:6).[82] However, from the moment of the first sin until today, truth has been assaulted and, as John Calvin once said, "Even a dog barks when his master is attacked."[83] Therefore, Christians must vigorously pursue truth and fight against lies. If a school does not encourage its students to pursue truth—or if students are unwilling to take a stand for the truth in the face of strong opposition—perhaps that school is not where Christians should be during their college years, especially since the only legitimate education is one that intersects at all points with the divine revelation of the living God.[84] After all, "if you don't get educated through the lens of Scripture, is that even an education?"[85]

---

81 *Merriam-Webster*, s.v. "Truth," accessed October 5, 2015, http://www.merriam-webster.com/dictionary/truth.

82 Notwithstanding this statement, there are times when it is prudent to remain silent (Matthew 7:6; Mark 14:61).

83 Richard Taylor Stevenson, *John Calvin the Statesman* (New York: Jennings & Graham, 1907), 164.

84 John MacArthur, "John MacArthur on Choosing a College," The Master's College, accessed April 13, 2015, https://www.youtube.com/watch?v=yWMI5HmpNPc.

85 John MacArthur, "Through them…to the World," The Master's College, accessed Au-

Does the School Celebrate Purity or Filth?[86]

God has provided a clear warning to those who practice, encourage, and celebrate immoral behavior. About them He says, "Though they know God's righteous decree that those who practice such things deserve to die, they not only do them but give approval to those who practice them" (Romans 1:32). They are further warned that "bad company ruins good morals" (1 Corinthians 15:33), and God has advised that His blessings flow to those who delight in His Word and who are not under the influence of the wicked (Psalm 1:1-3).[87] Since students typically dedicate four years of their young adult lives to the college experience, and since God has made grave pronouncements on those who practice or are overly influenced by evil, it is helpful to take a look at some real-life examples of the filth that is being offered in some secular colleges to the impressionable young people who attend.

- In the school-wide "Condom Olympics," students at the University of Arizona participate in educational activities such as a condom wrapped egg toss.[88]

- At prestigious Wellesley College, the women at the all-female school (now open to transgender students) get to feast their eyes on a realistic looking statue of a man sleep-walking in his underwear.[89]

- At Colombia University, a pornographic movie was filmed in

---

gust 5, 2015, http://www.masters.edu/media/banner/education-2015/.

86 In an effort to demonstrate the depth of immorality available at many secular institutions, the following discussion contains references to a number of courses and events that would not otherwise be fit for inclusion in a professional Christian book.

87 Abraham's nephew, Lot, serves as a warning since he voluntarily chose to place his family into the evil and influential city of Sodom. Although it has been said that the problem with Lot's wife was not that she was living in Sodom, but that Sodom was living in her, one cannot underestimate the attraction of that sinful city on her soul.

88 Katherine Timpf, "University of Arizona class requires students to participate in 'Condom Olympics,'" *Campus Reform*, accessed October 5, 2015, http://campusreform. org/?ID=5437.

89 Katherine Timpf, "Despite protest, women's college refuses to remove realistic statue of man sleeping in his underwear," *Campus Reform*, accessed October 5, 2015, http:// campusreform.org/?ID=5421.

the school library to fight "gender tension."[90]

- At the University of Chicago, the annual "sex week" on campus features the "Lascivious Ball," a dance where clothing is optional.[91]

- At the University of Tennessee, the annual "sex week" features a masturbation workshop, bondage experts, porn stars, and even an aphrodisiac cooking class.[92] This is in addition to another course that aims to address the question of when orgasms are a political act.[93]

- Montana State University students get to enjoy a "Latex and Lace Condom Fashion Show," which is probably as perverse as it sounds.[94]

- Northwestern University celebrates its own sex week with sex position cookies, with the student bakers invited to "get naughty."[95]

- Harvard's annual sex week offers a workshop entitled, "What in the Butt: Anal Sex 101," which, even more sadly, is sponsored by the Harvard Chaplains.[96]

---

90 Katherine Timpf, "Students film feminist porno in Columbia University library," Campus Reform, accessed October 5, 2015, http://campusreform.org/?ID=5414.

91 Katherine Timpf, "U of Chicago to host 'clothing optional' dance party in campus hall," *Campus Reform*, accessed October 5, 2015, http://campusreform.org/?ID=5403.

92 Katherine Timpf, "Public university spending at least $25,500 on Sex Week," *Campus Reform*, accessed October 5, 2015, http://campusreform.org/?ID=5413.

93 Katherin Timpf, "Public university Sex Week to teach masturbation, when orgasms are a 'political act,'" *Campus Reform*, accessed October 5, 2015, http://www.campusreform.org/?ID=5397.

94 Dionisopolous, Timothy. "Montana State University Set to Host 'Latex and Lace Condom Fashion Show,'" *Campus Reform*. Accessed October 5, 2015. http://campusreform.org/?ID=5376.

95 Katherine Timpf, "Northwestern Univ. College Feminists celebrated Sex Week with 'sex position cookies,'" *Campus Reform*, accessed October 5, 2015, http://campusreform.org/?ID=5369.

96 James Michael Nichols, "Harvard University Offers 'What What In The Butt: Anal Sex 101,'" *Huffington Post*, accessed October 5, 2015, http://www.huffingtonpost.com/2014/11/05/harvard-anal-sex-class_n_6102804.html; *see also* Sexual Health Education & Advocacy throughout Harvard College, "Sex Week at Harvard," *Hsexweek.org,* accessed

- Northwestern University's students in a psychology class were subject to a live sex demonstration in class.[97]

That the secular college experience involves such degrading activities should come as no surprise to those paying attention to higher education. In addition to the above activities, many colleges offer courses where students watch and even create their own pornography ("porn studies").[98] Yale, UCLA, Boston University, the University of Texas—the list goes on and on in terms of supposedly prestigious institutions that have become playgrounds for mankind's perversion.[99] In addition to the open sexual perversion available on secular campuses, it is difficult to find a secular college today that does not celebrate and welcome lifestyles that are an abomination to the almighty God.

For example, Duke University now approves gender-neutral housing for LGBTQAI students.[100] Another major university is now reported

---

November 10, 2014, http://www.hsexweek.org/schedule/.

97 Jessica Bennett, "Northwestern University's Live Sex Class," *The Daily Beast*, accessed September 14, 2015, http://www.thedailybeast.com/articles/2011/03/03/the-story-behind-northwestern-universitys-live-sex-class.html.

98 *See* Luke Gilkerson, "Porn 101: College Campuses Using Porn in the Classroom, *Covenant Eyes*, accessed September 17, 2015, http://www.covenanteyes.com/2008/10/31/porn-101-college-campuses-using-porn-in-the-classroom/ (discussing various pornography courses at such institutions as UCLA, MIT, UC Berkeley, Vanderbilt, New York University, Wesleyan, UC Santa Barbara, Virginia Tech); Jack Butler, "College Offers Course Devoted Entirely to Pornography," *The College Fix*, accessed September 17, 2015, http://www.thecollegefix.com/post/13039/ ; Michael Leahy, *Porn University: What college students are really saying about sex on campus* (Chicago, IL: Northfield Publishing, 2009).

99 Cynthia Hua, "Sex Week Planned for February," *Yale Daily News*, accessed September 14, 2015, http://yaledailynews.com/blog/2012/12/12/sex-week-planned-for-february/; UCLA Art & Global Health Center, "UCLA Sex Squad," *artglobalhealth.org,* accessed September 14, 2015, http://artglobalhealth.org/amp/uclasexsquad/; Sexual Empowerment and Awareness, "Schedule: Sex Week at University of Texas," *SexweekUT.org,* accessed November 10, 2014, http://sexweekut.org/schedule/; Sexual Health Education & Advocacy throughout Harvard College, "Sex Week at Harvard," *Hsexweek.org,* accessed October 5, 2015, http://www.hsexweek.org/schedule/; Boston University Student Health Services, "Frisky February: 28 Days of Stimulation," *Boston University,* accessed September 14, 2015, http://www.bu.edu/shs/wellness/wellness-programs/sexual/frisky-february-events/; Katherine Cusumano, "The Truth Laid Bare: Naked Donut Run Sweetens Reading Period," *The Brown Daily Herald*, accessed October 5, 2015, http://www.browndailyherald.com/2013/01/23/the-truth-laid-bare-naked-donut-run-sweetens-reading-period/; Caitlin Hardgrove, "Top College Traditions to do Before you Graduate," *Her Campus*, accessed September 15, 2015, http://www.hercampus.com/life/top-college-traditions-do-you-graduate.

100 Steven Larson, "Duke Approves Gender-Neutral Housing for Freshman to Accommo-

to advertise accommodations "for a grand total of 14 different gender identities."[101] Even the highly reputed University of California system offers students six choices to choose from when identifying their gender.[102] Although it is difficult to determine whether academia is leading the world down this dark path, or if it is the other way around, the wholesale abandonment of God's law has led to an ever-darkening of the human mind, to the point where those who celebrate evil actually proclaim that they are "a beacon, a light to the rest of the world."[103]

That said, Christian schools are not immune to the influence of the world. Many believing students struggle with pornography, others use alcohol or drugs, some engage in premarital sex, and a number violate various codes of conduct. The difference is that solid Christian schools have taken positions *against* these activities. They hold students accountable for their actions and have systems in place for discipline and counseling. Consequences for failing to turn from these behaviors range from suspension to expulsion. In short, purposefully Christian schools do not welcome the debauchery that is so prevalent and often celebrated on secular campuses.

So is there a difference between secular and Christian colleges? Yes. Does that difference matter? Yes. For the vast majority of believing students who are not mature enough to handle the folly that will be thrown at them on a daily basis on a secular campus, a Christian education is a far better choice. Put another way, it is a sad situation that parents find themselves in today. They claim to want the best for their children, and they are clearly warned to not contribute to their

---

date LGBTQAI Students," *Campus Reform,* accessed October 5, 2015, http://campusreform.org/?ID=5367
(These letters stand for the following: Lesbian, Gay, Bisexual, Transgender, Queer, Ally, and Intersex.)

101 David Gibson, "San Francisco Archbishop Salvatore Cordileone's Sad (But Predictable) Views on Caitlyn Jenner," *Huffington Post,* accessed June 4, 2015, http://www.huffingtonpost.com/2015/06/04/salvatore-cordileone-gender-ideology_n_7507638.html.

102 Fox News, "University of California offers six choices for 'gender identity,'" *Fox News,* accessed September 15, 2015, http://www.foxnews.com/us/2015/07/28/university-california-offers-six-choices-for-gender-identity/?intcmp=hpbt3.

103 Associated Press, "Ireland backs legalizing gay marriage by a landslide," *Fox News,* accessed September 15, 2015, http://www.foxnews.com/world/2015/05/23/ireland-gay-marriage/ (Cabinet Minister celebrating the fact that Ireland had become the first country in the world to enshrine gay marriage in its constitution).

stumbling (Luke 17:2); but many Christian parents actively push their kids to think in worldly terms when selecting a college and, by so doing, those kids end up attending schools where they are encouraged to indulge selfish, immoral desires, and they grow up into immorality and a false sense of adulthood. Unfortunately, most of those who travel this route never make it back to the narrow path, having been so tainted by the world's impurity and hollow worldview that the light that was once freely available has been replaced by a darkness that hardens the soul (Hebrews 3:13). Those who call evil good and vice versa (Isaiah 5:18-20)[104] are suppressing the truth (Romans 1:18). Their foolish hearts are darkened and they have been given over to their sinful desires (Romans 1:21, 24). Blessed is the man who sees this danger and avoids it, even during the college years (Proverbs 22:3).[105]

---

104 Apart from the sexual perversion being celebrated on college campuses, it is difficult to trust that professors will teach core subjects in an unbiased and morally neutral manner. *See, e.g.,* Gregg Jarrett, "What are college professors (not) teaching?" *Fox News*, accessed September 15, 2015, http://www.foxnews.com/opinion/2014/10/14/what-are-college-pro-fessors-not-teaching/?intcmp=features (discussing the liberal failure to acknowledge facts and citing the ever-increasing figure of over 60% of college professors who self-identify as liberal or "far left" as compared to only 12% who identify as conservative); Mark Osler, "The 5 Scariest Teachings of Jesus," *Huffington Post*, accessed September 15, 2015, http://www.huffingtonpost.com/mark-osler/scariest-teachings-of-jesus_b_6075490.html?ncid=tx-tlnkusaolp00000592 (law professor purporting to analyze Scripture and claiming that Jesus' apostles abandoned their families and further specifying that Peter probably left his wife "impoverished and overwhelmed when he abandoned her"); Fox News, "College Prof Makes Students Recite Anti-American 'Pledge of Allegiance," *Fox News*, accessed September 14, 2015, http://www.foxnews.com/us/2014/12/08/college-prof-makes-students-re-cite-anti-american-pledge-allegiance/ (college professor requiring his students to memo-rize and recite an anti-American pledge). *But see* Steve Golden, "Creation on Campus," *Answers*, October-December 2014, 74-79 (although creationism is not taught well in most schools, there are some that at least teach various points of view in a respectful manner).

105 To those who think this perverse teaching is a passing fad or can easily be avoided in college, this author has personal experience from attending a major public university 25 years ago. Ignoring my parents' advice, I enrolled in a human sexuality course to fulfill a liberal arts course requirement. To this day, I cannot erase from my mind the perverse im-ages that I was exposed to during that course, and I know that it was one step down a dark path I traveled during that time. Only by God's grace did He determine to save me through His loving discipline (Proverbs 3:11-12). Sadly, the world has only gotten worse since that time and conduct that in the past was regarded as perverse is now considered normal *See* Johnson, foreword to *Total Truth*, by Pearcey, 13.

CHAPTER 8

THE DANGERS OF MAKING
THE WRONG CHOICE

This book began with a description of the ingredients of a college experience, all of which combine to deeply influence a young person's life. Indeed, in light of the training and influence received by a student during the college years, it is no surprise that college selection—and the choices made during college—carry consequences well into the adult life (and eternity). Not only can a choice of college influence a course of study and a subsequent job search, but a student on his own for the first time will be required to make independent decisions on coursework, friendships, morality, and faith. The selection of a spouse during the college years likely will result in children, who will have their own children, and so on. Each of these individuals has an individual soul, accountable to God. The strengthening or weakening of one's faith during this four-year period also will carry consequences. Some will advance in their faith as God desires, while others will flounder, requiring years and years of struggle to move past poor decision-making habits learned at school. In sum, decisions have consequences, which is why Scripture is to be consulted in all things—even for college choice.

As the title of this chapter implies, I believe that for the vast majority of Christian students there is a "right" choice in terms of deciding between a Christian and non-Christian college education. (*Christian,* in case I've not been clear.) In fact, even among various acceptable options, one of them often is "better" than the others when it comes to analyzing which school selection likely will result in improving one's walk with and knowledge of God. For example, if a student is considering two schools, an objective, honest assessment typically can result in a wise determination as to which of the two is the better choice, even if each is acceptable. However, it is impossible to lay down the law on college selection for every individual. Specifically, a line should not be drawn where God has not drawn one first; a rule should not be invented where God has not made one. Every Christian must make his own decision—based on his own conscience—after much prayer and after consulting Scripture and other believers (*see* Romans 14).

Some might think this discussion takes the college selection process too seriously. They might argue that choosing a school is not a life or death decision. Those in the spiritual realm would disagree. Believers are in a constant state of spiritual battle, and refusing to consider whether an educational choice will lead to a softening of Christian defenses ignores the realities presented in the Bible (Ephesians 6:12; 2 Corinthians 10:3-5; Romans 8:38-39). Indeed, believers are instructed to be spiritually vigilant at all times (including when choosing a school and during the college years), because even if the spirit is willing, the flesh is weak (Matthew 26:41).

Nothing written herein should be interpreted as advancing the idea that a true believer can lose his salvation. That is not the point. In fact, Scripture teaches that God's children know and follow Him, and that no one will snatch them out of God's hand (John 10:27-28; Romans 8:1). Humans are saved by grace through faith, not through their own effort, even while in college. "For by grace you have been saved through faith. And this is not your own doing; it is the gift of God, not a result of works, so that no one may boast. For we are his workmanship, created in Christ Jesus for good works, which God prepared beforehand, that we should walk in them" (Ephesians 2:8-10). So while it is important to consider God's glory when choosing a school, His ways will not be thwarted, no matter the choice (Job 42:2).

With the above in mind, Christian parents and students should consider at least two issues when planning for the future. First, is the student really a Christian? The Bible instructs individuals to engage in self-examination to ensure that saving faith is present: "Examine yourselves, to see whether you are in the faith. Test yourselves. Or do you not realize this about yourselves, that Jesus Christ is in you?—unless indeed you fail to meet the test!" (2 Corinthians 13:5). One evidence of true faith is whether or not the individual is obedient to God's commands (John 14:23-24; James 2:18). If a student goes off to college and systematically follows the world's sinful path without coming to repentance, chances are that he is not saved.[106] At many secular colleges, there is very little Christian influence to draw such an unbelieving individual to Christ (1 Corinthians 15:33). In one sense, it certainly is *safer* to be at a Christian school where God's Word is taught and honored because failure to genuinely accept Christ is a life or death choice—for eternity.

Second, although a true Christian will not be lost for eternity, that same person can be rendered spiritually ineffective by sin and can, by his failure to use his talents for God's kingdom, lose out on eternal rewards. For example, the Bible warns that he who walks in the flesh is spiritually immature, like an infant (1 Corinthians 3:1). Every believer is called to put off immoral living (Colossians 3:5) and to put on godly characteristics (Colossians 3:12-14). The one who does not grow in the faith will not be in a position to be used as a pure tool for God's righteousness. In fact, his stagnation might be such that he loses his influence on others and becomes such a watered-down Christian that the name of God will be impugned and non-believers will be confused. Such a person will not be one through whom God's Word will be preached (Romans 10:14). Additionally, that same person who is not obeying God or passing sound doctrine on to others, "will suffer loss, though he himself will be saved, but only as through fire" (1 Corinthians 3:15). Losing out on eternal rewards *is* a very big deal, especially because the Creator of the universe is the one handing out the rewards. In light of the risk of being rendered an ineffective witness for Christ and losing out on God's sweet heavenly gifts, it is easy to see that choosing to place oneself in an influential environment—such as a college that encourages selfish living—likely would be a dangerous proposition.

Additionally, there is yet another reason why making the wrong college choice can have devastating results. A student might have his faith weakened by serial attacks on it from those he encounters at school. What if the first professor a student encounters at college is an atheist, Marxist, feminist, or homosexual who considers it his job to force Christian students to reject their faith? What if he requires conformity

---

106 Scripture also teaches that there will be those who appear to walk in the faith, yet will fall away and be cast into outer darkness because they never truly knew the Lord (Matthew 7:21-23).

to certain non-Christian principles to pass his class? What if he takes it upon himself to display pornographic images or use vulgar language during lectures? Or what if he makes a mockery of the student by walking him through a series of questions designed to make his faith look idiotic?[107]

Unless the new student is already well-versed in apologetics (the use of reasoned arguments to justify religious belief), he may fall victim to the professor's tactics. Although there may be some recourse by appealing to the school administration, most students will either not want to risk further loss or embarrassment in a public administrative battle with a tenured professor, or the appeals process might be so protracted as to be ineffective. In reality, most 18-year-old students are not mature enough to debate with professors or understand hidden agendas.[108]

The tragedy of lost or weakened faith during college is not invented by youth pastors intent on ushering all kids into ministry, nor is there data to prove that professors are solely to blame. But the trend of weak and ineffective Christian living is borne out by the numbers. For example, once they attend college, a huge percentage of students

---

107 "Freshmen usually are intimidated by college professors. The tsunami of information in classes made it difficult to think through the subject matter. A number of students had likable and intelligent professors who 'refused to tolerate students' beliefs as viable' and actively sought to change their convictions. The lack of a commensurate input of spiritual truth began a slide away from faith." Bill Brown, "Top 10 Challenges Christian Students Face in College," *Cedarville University*, accessed September 22, 2015, https://www.cedarville.edu/eNews/ParentPrep/2012/Challenges-Christian-Students-Face-in-College.aspx.

108 In the words of one author, "We would never send out missionaries who are insufficiently trained and prepared to deal with the false religions and temptations of another culture. OK, I'm going to say it: I think no young person should be sent to a secular college— or for that matter many 'Christian' colleges—unless he is exceptionally knowledgeable of the Scriptures, is leading a strong Christian life, knows how to resist peer pressure and resist temptation to sex and drugs. (Many Christian kids go off to college and by the second term lose their virginity. Premarital sex is normal on most campuses, even some Christian campuses.) If he is not prepared to question his professors and if he may give in to their skepticism and attacks on the Christian faith, he does not belong there. If we want our children to lose their faith, there are less expensive ways to help them do that! (I'm being deliberately sarcastic to make an important point.)" Randy Alcorn, "Choosing a Christian College or Secular University," *Eternal Perspectives Ministries*, accessed April 16, 2015, http://www.epm.org/blog/2009/Aug/19/question-and-answer-of-the-week-choosing-a-christi.

reject the faith they claimed prior to enrollment.[109] In fact, most faith change occurs during the first year away from home.[110] These statistics are in addition to other noteworthy views held by students, such as the fact that almost 80% of female college students consider themselves "feminists," although 26% of those did *not* hold that belief prior to college, and approximately 75% of female students believe women should have a right to an abortion.[111] The point is that college is a place where students *will be influenced*.[112] The question is whether that influence will be godly or not, and whether it will work to increase one's faith or not. Choosing a college is serious business. As theologian John Owen (1616-1683) warned, believers must "be killing sin or it will be killing you."[113] This is especially true during the formative college years when the risk is great, which is why the Devil prowls around like a roaring lion looking for someone to devour (1 Peter 5:8). To him, "the corpse of an enemy always smells sweet."[114]

---

109 John Stonestreet and Chuck Edwards, "Students Abandoning the Faith," *Summit Ministries*, accessed October 7, 2015, http://www.summit.org/resources/essays/students-abandoning-the-faith/.

110 Henderson, "Investing in Their Faith."

111 Julie Pennell, "What College Students Really Think About Feminism," *Teen Vogue*, accessed July 13, 2015, https://www.yahoo.com/style/what-college-students-really-think-about-feminism-123750899955.html.

112 In the movie, *Miracle on 34th Street*, Kris Kringle asks the young Macy's employee about his recent visit to the company psychologist: "Alfred—what else has he found wrong with you?" Alfred replies, "Oh, nothing much. Just that I hate my father. I didn't know it, but he says I do." This humorous exchange highlights one of the problems of sitting at the feet of someone who is wise in the world's eyes. The authority figure can plant subversive ideas that would not sway a more mature person. *Miracle on 34th Street*, directed by Seaton, George (Twentieth Century Fox Film Corporation, 1947), DVD (20th Century Fox Home Entertainment, 2006).

113 John Owen, *Of The Mortification of Sin in Believers* (1656), in *Overcoming Sin & Temptation*, ed. Kelly Kapic and Justin Taylor (Wheaton, IL: Crossway Books, 2006), 50.

114 Kevin Kiley, "Thumbing through the Napoleonic Wars: The Words of Napoleon and Others Who May Have Influenced His Methods," *The Napoleon Series,* accessed October 5, 2015, http://www.napoleon-series.org/research/napoleon/c_quotes.html. There are many examples of individuals raised in Christian families who were so infected by secular liberalism that they rejected traditional teachings of the Christian faith. Some did not go quietly into spiritual oblivion, however, but caused extensive damage to the name of Christ that they still carried. One example is found in German theologian, Friedrich Schleiermacher (1768-1834), who attended a university where he was exposed to the thinking of unbelieving skeptics who exalted human reason above all else. He soon denied his faith, and gave rise to a form of religious belief that called itself "Christian," but denied the authority of the Bible. This type of thinking, in turn, gave rise to various other forms of theological liberalism, such as the social gospel (de-emphasizing personal sin and the need for a savior and,

Stay away from his snare (Proverbs 29:25; 2 Timothy 2:26) and do not render unto the world that which is God's.[115]

instead, focusing on ethical conduct in society) and the charismatic movement (emphasizing personal experience over the power of and need for God's written Word). John MacArthur, *Strange Fire* (Nashville, TN: Nelson Books, 2013), 215-217; Brian Gerrish, *A Prince of the Church: Schleiermacher and the Beginnings of Modern Theology* (Philadelphia: Fortress Press, 1984), 25. In sum, the potential damage that false instruction can cause to the individual and to the church as a whole is enormous and should not be underestimated.

115 *See generally* John MacArthur, "We will not bow," *Grace to You*, accessed September 28, 2015, http://www.gty.org/resources/sermons/80-425/we-will-not-bow.

CHAPTER 9

PARENT INVOLVEMENT
IN THE COLLEGE CHOICE

PARENTS ARE WELL-POSITIONED
TO PROVIDE WISE COUNSEL

At this point, the role of believing parents in helping their young adult children choose a college must be addressed. Not only are parents potentially best positioned to know the strengths and weaknesses of their children, but the most common college experience involves relying on at least some of mom and dad's money to help with the cost. Further, choosing a college without seeking parental input is foolish, and God warns against making plans without such consultation (Proverbs 15:22). All believers are part of the Body of Christ, so a primary goal for every believer is to help other believers be built up for the benefit of the Body as a whole (as opposed to in isolation or merely seeking one's personal interests; Philippians 2:3-5). As Paul put it, "if all were a single member, where would the body be?" (1 Corinthians 12:19). To be more specific, the wise student will seek his parents' advice, and wise parents will assist in the process, with God's glory and the entire Body of Christ in mind. Helping a college bound student choose a school where he will best be built up as a believer is simply an extension of the biblical process of raising kids and preparing them for adulthood when they will influence others for the Body of Christ.[116] As one author put it, "Children are the living messages we send to a time we will not see."[117] Parents should endeavor to ensure that those messages are love letters to the Almighty, even

---

116 Parental involvement contemplates more than just the parent seeking to satisfy a college bound child's demands. Although many modern-day parents have abandoned their duty, the Bible is clear that parents are required to bring their children up in the fear and admonition of the Lord (Ephesians 6:4). This requires parents to consider the *holiness* of their children, not just their happiness. Choosing the right place to study can result in an increase in both. *See* Tommy Mitchell, "Should Creation Be Taught in Public Schools?" *Answers*, October-December 2014, 94; *see also* Psalm 127:4.

117 Neil Postman, *The Disappearance of Childhood* (New York: Delacorte Press, 1982), xi.

while recognizing that repentance, faith, and salvation are entirely the work of the Holy Spirit.

Train Up a Child

When children are little, they are warned against the dangers of strangers. Small children are notoriously gullible and parents are rightly concerned to warn them of the risks associated with making bad decisions and believing lies. God gives His children the same warning. "Little children, let no one deceive you" (1 John 3:7). The idea is to not allow anyone to lead believers astray. In conveying these words, John was taking on the parental role, teaching his spiritual children to not be fooled by those who say they are righteous but who do not live righteously. John serves as a good example to all believing parents who seek to direct the paths of their children.

In speaking to the command, warning, and general truth in Scripture that parents are to "train up a child in the way he should go; even when he is old he will not depart from it" (Proverbs 22:6), Bishop J.C. Ryle (1816-1900) stated that the reason the vast majority of children do not walk with God as adults is because, "The Lord's commandment in our text is not regarded; and therefore the Lord's promise in our text is not fulfilled."[118] "Children are born with a decided bias toward evil, and therefore if you let them choose for themselves, they are certain to choose wrong."[119] In order to help them choose wisely, parents must remember that "their minds are like a lump of metal— not to be forged and made useful at once, but only by a succession of little blows."[120] The idea is to teach them, line by line, little by little, God's commands. These commands provide a basis for these children to be well-grounded and not waverers. They need to be trained to read the Bible consistently and with reverence; they need to learn to pray; they need to understand the value of fellowship; and they need to

---

118 J.C. Ryle, "The Duties of Parents," *WholesomeWords.org*, accessed March 12, 2015, http://www.wholesomewords.org/etexts/ryle/ryleduties.pdf, first published in *The Upper Room: Being Truths for the Times* (London: William Hunt & Co., 1888)).

119 Ibid.

120 Ibid. Notably, there are two interpretations of this verse (an instruction to train a child in the ways of the Lord, or a warning not to allow a child to become set *in accordance with his way*, according to his natural, sinful bent). Either reading should cause Christian parents to administer wise counsel, loving admonishment, and godly discipline.

learn to be truth-tellers empowered by the Holy Spirit. Such righteous behavior does not come naturally. It is learned, mostly by watching others. "Children learn more by the eye than they do by the ear."[121] That is why it is said that he who sins in the presence of a child, "sins double."[122]

In the not too distant past, teenagers would not necessarily have been categorized as children. In fact, the word teenager apparently was coined only in the early 1940s in a *Reader's Digest* article.[123] Before then, those approaching their twenties were considered adults (perhaps occasioned by a shorter life expectancy, a need to work to support the family, or simply a lack of self-centered leisure activities that encourage perpetual immaturity). Now, however, college-aged students are still, in many respects, children. They rely on their parents for financial support, many have never held formal employment, and they lack real world experience. When compared to past generations of Christians, most have a limited understanding of the Bible. In short, they still are in need of training. For many of these young people, college is the transition step to adulthood, and a place where they can receive training "in the way [they] should go" (Proverbs 22:6).[124] Or, put another way, college is a place where the warning to *not* follow their sinful bent can be reinforced.

As explained above, college can be a place not only for vocational training, but also for moral discipline. If you are a Christian parent who is involved in the selection of a college for your child, perhaps you have not focused on these issues. However, you probably have given at least some thought about what you want for your offspring. It is not a sin to want your child to be financially comfortable. It is not wrong to want him to be in a stable marriage and to have healthy children of his own. And it is not even wrong to desire that he live a long, healthy life. However, the ultimate goal should be that your children become more and more like Christ, being conformed to his

---

121 Ryle, "The Duties of Parents."

122 Ibid.

123 Alex Harris and Brett Harris, *Do Hard Things* (Colorado Springs, CO: Multnomah Books, 2008), 29-30.

124 This lack of training is especially disappointing in light of clear scriptural commands to teach children the way of the Lord (Deuteronomy 6:4-9).

image through the power of the Holy Spirit as God imparts wisdom through Scripture. The college selection process should maintain this goal in view.

Some parents, however, think of their kids as already being "ready" for the world. The words of the apostle Paul should serve as a warning: "Therefore let anyone who thinks that he stands take heed lest he fall" (1 Corinthians 10:12). In other words, to the extent a parent thinks that a college-aged student is already established in his beliefs and that the college experience will not cause him to "depart" from the faith, that parent should consider the following statistics.

Of incoming college freshmen, well over 50% who call themselves born-again Christians upon entering a public university no longer identify themselves in that way four years later or, if they do, they have not attended church services in more than a year. This rate of rejection is even higher at private secular colleges and worse at Catholic colleges. In fact, similar patterns of rejection occur at all types of institutions *except* for students attending colleges that are purposefully Christian.[125]

Although there are many schools that call themselves "Christian," the institutions that experience the largest *drop-offs* from faith include the following: private secular colleges, state colleges, colleges associated with the Presbyterian denomination, and Catholic affiliated institutions. In comparison, those that experience the largest *increases* in overall religious commitment include Protestant colleges, Baptist colleges, and those affiliated with the Protestant movement. The findings in one secular study stated it as follows: "As expected, attending an 'evangelical' college is associated with generally positive patterns of spiritual growth, while attending a public college or university is associated with larger-than-average declines in self-rated spirituality."[126] Further, those who attend colleges that are members of the Council for Christian Colleges and Universities (CCCU) demonstrate significantly higher religious commitment than students

---

125 Henderson, "Investing in Their Faith."
126 Astin and Astin, "Spirituality in Higher Education."

at non-CCCU institutions.[127] Unlike other schools, CCCU member institutions adhere to Christian principles and hire believers as full-time faculty. They often require chapel attendance and prioritize discipleship.[128]

These figures, while sad, should not be surprising. Most of the post high school "faith" fallout is a reflection of unregenerate hearts that finally have the opportunity to choose for themselves. Furthermore, typical secular colleges do not emphasize Scripture reading, church attendance, or faith. A significant transition often takes place during the college years and the young adults who enter school move from depending on and being somewhat controlled by parents to being independent adults. They move from a faith that they feel is imposed on them to a situation where they must own their faith.[129] In these circumstances, the major changes that students undergo during college can be drastic if not girded with the truth and if the faith they grew up with is constantly under attack from other students and professors. In fact, over a decade ago, 75% of American college seniors indicated in a poll that their professors do not teach right or wrong, but instead, they teach that right and wrong "depend on differences in individual values and cultural diversity."[130] In this age of progressive cultural relativism, that figure probably is much higher today. In short, parents cannot count on secular college professors to "train up a child in the way he should go" (Proverbs 22:6). That is a privilege and obligation borne by parents.

---

127 Henderson, "Investing in Their Faith."

128 Ibid., "Investing in Their Faith." Sadly, the CCCU recently has been embroiled in a controversy that appears to evidence the organization's willingness to accept or affiliate with schools that do not embrace biblical principles. If this trend continues, it is doubtful that CCCU institutions will have a noticeably different student body from secular schools, and a corresponding drop-off of students of faith will follow. *See* J.C. Derrick, "Two Schools Leave CCCU—For Opposite Reasons," *Worldmag.org,* accessed January 26, 2016, http://www.worldmag.com/2015/12/two_schools_leave_cccu_for_opposite_reasons; Ken Ham, "Ken Ham Praises John MacArthur's Master's College For Leaving Association That Rejects Biblical Creation," *Worldview Weekend*, accessed January 26, 2016, http://www.worldviewweekend.com/news/article/ken-ham-praises-john-macarthurs-masters-college-leaving-association-rejects-biblical.

129 Henderson, "Investing in Their Faith."

130 Pearcey, *Total Truth*, 113; *see* John Leo, "Professors Who See No Evil," *Aish.com*, accessed September 16, 2015, http://www.aish.com/sp/ph/48923192.html.

"But I Want My Independence!"

Every person has experienced it. Most teenagers, however, seem to struggle with keeping it inside. They want their independence. They want to make their own decisions. They want to control their destiny and if mistakes are to be made, they want to make them on their own. Instead of hiding this desire, they voice their desperation: "I want to be free! Stop trying to control me!" These feelings are similar to the words from the song *Let it Go* from the hit movie *Frozen*, "It's time to see what I can do, to test the limits and break through, no right, no wrong, no rules for me, I'm free!"[131] In short, teenagers often are oblivious to the dangers of reckless abandon and impervious to the wisdom that comes from the input of older people, including parents. This pride of an independent spirit primarily expresses itself in two areas—resistance to authority and an unteachable attitude.[132] In simple words, many teenagers are know-it-alls and do not want to be told what to do.

Teens sometimes seek to avoid or reject their parents' counsel on college choice and, instead, they foolishly listen to their friends who talk about college as if it is a fanciful, independent place where nothing bad will ever happen, no matter how cavalier the attitude toward the lusts of the flesh. In Tom Wolfe's book, *I am Charlotte Simmons,* the main character's friend aptly summarizes what she has learned with a series of questions and answers:

> I guess what I really mean is college is like this four-year period you have when you can try anything—*everything*—and if it goes wrong, there's no consequences? You know what I mean? Nobody's keeping score? You can do things that if you tried them before you got to college, your family would be crying and pulling their hair out and giving you these now-see-what-you've-gone-and-done looks? College is the only time in your life, or your adult life anyway, when you can really *experiment*, and at a certain point,

---

131 Kristen Anderson-Lopez and Robert Lopez, "Let it Go," *Frozen: The Songs*, Disney, 2014, CD.

132 Jerry Bridges, *Respectable Sins* (Colorado Springs, CO: NavPress 2007), 97.

when you graduate or whatever, everybody's memory like evaporates. You tried this and this and this and this, and you learned a lot about how things are, but nobody's gonna remember it? It's like amnesia, totally, and there's no record, and you leave college exactly the way you came in, pure as rainwater.[133]

In this western culture that celebrates narcissistic self-image and individuality, most people don't understand that this desire for independence and a "free pass" is unbiblical and unrealistic. "Whoever loves discipline loves knowledge, but he who hates reproof is stupid" (Proverbs 12:1). Sin is the root of this self-centered, independent attitude. Take, for example, God's plan for sanctification. He has given His children three sources of help in this process:

- The Holy Spirit, "But the Helper, the Holy Spirit, whom the Father will send in my name, he will teach you all things and bring to your remembrance all that I have said to you" (John 14:26).

- The Bible, "Your word is a lamp to my feet and a light to my path" (Psalm 119:105).

- Other believers, "... not neglecting to meet together, as is the habit of some, but encouraging one another, and all the more as you see the Day drawing near" (Hebrews 10:25).

God did not design humans to live a solitary existence or to be independent. In fact, humans are purposefully designed to be *dependent* on God for everything from breath to eternal life (Genesis 2:7; John 15:5; John 6:47-50). Unfortunately, however, most teenagers who think of independence at college as "freedom" do not recognize that they simply are becoming more and more enslaved to their own sinful natures (Galatians 5).[134]

---

133 Tom Wolfe, *I am Charlotte Simmons* (New York: Farrar, Straus and Giroux, 2004), 157.

134 "As one freshman put it, 'I feel like God dropped me off at college and said, 'I'll be back to pick you up in four years.'" Note that this student, like many of his peers, planned to be picked up when he graduated—in the same place and by the same driver. It is not that his religious identity was unimportant (quite the contrary), only that he did not see its relevancy to his college education and campus experience." Tim Clydesdale, "Abandoned, Pursued, or Safely Stowed? The Religious Life of First Year Undergraduates," (Social Science Research

In fact, to many young people, their feelings or opinions are authoritative. Even when confronted with direct scriptural references, they respond with how they "feel" or what they "think." "There is no willingness to grapple with the teaching of Scripture."[135] In so doing, they tacitly reject biblical mandates to keep God's commandments (Proverbs 3:1); to not forget the teaching of parents (Proverbs 3:1; 4:1); to be attentive to wisdom (Proverbs 5:1); and to treasure God's commands (Proverbs 7:1).[136] So, despite their pleas for freedom, they still need training so that when they are old, they "will not depart from it" (Proverbs 22:6).

With that in mind, parents and students should understand what the major influences in a student's life will be for the next four years, since they will have direct impact on a student's thoughts, feelings, and actions. These influences include professors, textbooks, classmates, friends, roommates, campus organizations, entertainment, and social activities. For example, a student might read an assigned book and formulate thoughts, discuss it with other students over lunch, listen to a professor provide his insight, and then combine all of the above into an essay that solidifies his thinking on the subject. Or he might hang out at a party with friends on the weekend, being encouraged to participate in their activities or meet some of their friends, all the while discussing issues they think are important and sizing up friends and acquaintances in order to evaluate who to spend time with during the next weeks or months or years. Even campus organizations have certain goals and hold events that can impact a student's thinking and behavior. These influences can be either good or bad. The wise decision maker will make an effort to consider the quality of that influence *prior* to being subjected to it (Proverbs 13:20; 22:3).

So what does this look like for a parent who is ready to release his child into the hands of a college? If it is concluded that the child is still in need of significant spiritual maturation, and to the extent the parent can influence where his child will attend college, he should consider

---

Council Essay, October 9, 2006), 2, cited in Fuller Youth Institute, "You Make the Call: What College Freshmen Need to Hear from their Youth Pastors," *Sticky Faith*, accessed September 22, 2015, http://stickyfaith.org/articles/you-make-the-call.

135 Bridges, *Respectable Sins*, 98.

136 Ibid.

the passages in Scripture that warn against causing another believer to stumble. "But whoever causes one of these little ones who believe in me to sin, it would be better for him to have a great millstone fastened around his neck and to be drowned in the depth of the sea" (Matthew 18:6; Malachi 2:8). More specifically, if a believing parent determines that his child is easily influenced, and especially if the child is not yet firm in his faith and may fall victim to unrighteous influence (whether it comes in the form of a professor, textbook, or friend), then the parent *must* do whatever he can to equip the student for these battles as well as to protect him against unnecessary conflict by directing the malleable child to righteous training. The wise parent should consider who will be teaching his child at school. "But woe to you, scribes and Pharisees, hypocrites! For you shut the kingdom of heaven in people's faces. For you neither enter yourselves nor allow those who would enter to go in. Woe to you, scribes and Pharisees, hypocrites! For you travel across sea and land to make a single proselyte, and when he becomes a proselyte, you make him twice as much a child of hell as yourselves" (Matthew 23:13-15). In other words, many young adults (old children) still need significant training in righteousness. They should not be directed to a place that will abdicate that responsibility, and they certainly should not be subjected to influential teachers who seek to make them children of hell by teaching them to reject God's Word.

In sum, most Christian parents *should* be involved in the college selection process.[137] They still play a role in the spiritual upbringing of their children, and college can be an extension of parental beliefs and teachings. Neglecting that responsibility either by ignoring their kids' spiritual condition or by failing to help analyze potential schools may be tantamount to not finishing the task of raising children in the way they should go. And for those children who want to deny their Christian parents the ability to speak on the issue of school choice, they are wrong and should turn away from pride and foolishness (Proverbs 3:7; 11:2). As difficult as it might be for children to admit, sometimes parents really do know best. And parents, of course (who were once children a long time ago), should be compassionate and gracious in how they communicate their thoughts on the issue of college choice (Psalm 103:8; Ephesians 4:32).

---

137 In consultation with other believers, including the student's pastor/elders.

CHAPTER 10

BEING A GOOD STEWARD

THE NUMBERS GAME

Imagine a caretaker being entrusted with an amazing house to watch while the owner is away on a long trip. Instead of taking care of the premises for the owner, the caretaker moves in, piles dishes in the sink, lets dust accumulate everywhere, allows the plants and lawn to die, neglects the paint to the point where it starts to chip off the walls, and even takes out a loan on the house so that he can use the owner's equity for his own personal expenditures. Then imagine the day when the homeowner returns, only to find the caretaker napping in the master bedroom, still wearing muddy shoes that had been tracked through the house and surrounded by old pizza boxes and rubbish. The punishment for this employee would be severe and well deserved.

You might be wondering what this story has to do with choosing a college. If you claim the name of Jesus Christ as your Lord, this story has much to do with that decision. You are a steward of *all* the resources that God has entrusted to you, meaning, you are akin to "a person whose job is to manage the land and property of another person."[138] Those resources include your mind, your body, and your finances, all of which God has allowed you to use in this lifetime. Further, if you are a parent, one of the most valuable "assets" entrusted to you is your child. Are you training that child in the way he should go? (Proverbs 22:6). Are you using everything God has given you for the benefit of the King? Are you managing everything in such a way as to achieve a high return on His investment for His glory? Or are you using the Master's assets solely for your benefit and personal pleasure, while at the same time displaying a nonchalant attitude toward your God-given responsibilities? In short, are you the lazy caretaker who is living for himself without regard to the day when the Master returns?

---

138 *Merriam-Webster*, s.v. "Steward," accessed October 5, 2015, http://www.merriam-webster.com/dictionary/steward.

Jesus gave the clearest illustration of these responsibilities in the parable of the talents. In his story, Jesus told of three servants being given something of value by their master before he went on a trip (Matthew 25:14-30). Upon his return, he rewarded the first two servants who had invested his money and achieved a return on that investment. However, the third servant—who had done nothing with the money except return it without any increase—was called a "wicked and slothful servant." His failure to use the asset for his master's gain resulted in his being cast into the outer darkness where "there will be weeping and gnashing of teeth."

For believers wrestling with the college choice, there are at least three considerations that come to mind when considering Jesus' parable as well as the caretaker's story: children, mind, and money.

Children Must Be Invested Wisely

Children are a gift from God (Psalm 127:3), and parents are to care for and raise those children in the fear and admonition of the Lord (Ephesians 6:4; Deuteronomy 6:4-9). When selecting a college for a child, parents must think of a child as a "talent" that God wants invested for His glory. After all, He did not put children into the care of believing parents for them to be raised as if there were no hope for their souls, as enemies of the Almighty. In fact, God's Word is to be entrusted to faithful men (2 Timothy 2:2), and from the perspective of finite, human parents, every child has the opportunity to become one of those faithful people.[139] Invest in them wisely so that they have the opportunity to grow into an even greater investment for the kingdom, thus making wise investments in their own children someday. In one sense, God's plan is the ultimate, holy, pyramid scheme that allows participants to store up actual and eternal value in this life and the next by faithful living (1 Timothy 4:7-8).

The Mind Must Be Invested Wisely

Second, God has provided every person with a mind, so the question is this: How does God intend that His children develop and care for

---

139 Of course, salvation is of the Lord and is subject to His sovereign will (Romans 9:22-23).

the mind, especially knowing that without God's saving work, the mind is darkened, depraved, hostile, and blinded to the things of God? (Psalm 51:5; 1 Corinthians 2:14; Romans 8:7). While it must be acknowledged that not every professor at every secular institution teaches in a manner overtly hostile to Christianity, believers should ask whether their mental development should come at the feet of those who are opposed to God and His Word, or are there circumstances where the mind should be developed with and at the feet of fellow believers? Although every decision is personal and should be based on the application of God's Word to specific circumstances, Scripture provides good counsel to consider.

Specifically, God advises, "Above all else, guard your heart [mind][140] for everything you do flows from it" (Proverbs 4:23, *NIV*). If one aspect of the "talent" that God has provided includes the mind, and if the mind will be impacted in any way during the college years, believers will *not* be investing this talent wisely if they knowingly and voluntarily submit their minds to the influential filth of the world. It is not an overstatement to say that failing to guard one's mind in this regard is sin because it goes against this specific command of God. There is a direct correlation between what goes into a mind and actual conduct. "Everything" believers do flows directly from the mind (Proverbs 4:23). And what is inside is what actually defiles a person (Mark 7:20-23). When considering the impact of worldly influence on a person's behavior, modern phraseology comes in handy: "Garbage in, garbage out." Accordingly, the wise believer will consider what will be going into his mind during his four-year college stay and will take steps to ensure that it will not influence him to evil.[141]

---

140 The mind is often referred to as the "heart" in Scripture (*e.g.*, Hebrews 4:12; Psalm 119:11; Romans 1:21).

141 As set forth elsewhere in this book, this is not to say that every godly person will cave in to the temptation and influence of ungodly instruction. For this reason, I have repeatedly used the term "influential" when I write of ungodly instruction and input. There are believers who are able to guard their hearts and minds, through the power of the Holy Spirit, while being subjected to pagan teaching. (Daniel and his friends are good examples from Scripture; *see* Daniel 1.) They are not influenced to wickedness. However, the examples in Scripture of this occurring tend to involve circumstances where believers were forced into situations, as opposed to 21st century students who voluntarily choose a residential college experience for themselves. That being said, the question is whether the student will be influenced to sin, or whether he will influence others for Christ. While there are general assumptions that can be made in this regard, the analysis is person specific.

Money Must Be Invested Wisely

Third, God has entrusted parents with a certain amount of money and at least some of it will be spent on children (2 Corinthians 12:14, "Children are not obligated to save up for their parents, but parents for their children"). If those expenditures involve college, parents must consider where that God-given money should be spent. If the goal is to have an eternal impact and use God's money to advance His kingdom, why not direct college funds to soul-changing instruction?

Recent surveys show that a "moderate" college budget is approximately $23,000 for in-state tuition at a state public college (and close to double that amount for out-of-state tuition), and $46,000 for a private college.[142] That means that an average four-year public university experience will cost about $100,000 and an average four-year private university experience will amount to approximately $200,000. In the United States, the median annual income is approximately $41,000.[143] While some make more and some make less (oftentimes depending on level of education completed), the point is that even a moderate college budget can easily drain a savings account.[144]

In light of the significant expenditure required for a four-year college degree, it is helpful to read how others in the Christian faith have wrestled with money. For example, John Wesley asked himself four questions before spending money:

---

142 College Data, What's the Price Tag for a College Education?" *College Data*.com, accessed May 1, 2015, http://www.collegedata.com/cs/content/content_payarticle_tmpl.jhtml?articleId=10064; *see also* Brian Kelly, "Is College Still Worth It?" *U.S. News & World Report*, September 2010, 8.

143 Lam Thy Vo, "What Americans Earn," *Planet Money,* accessed May 1, 2015, http://www.npr.org/blogs/money/2012/07/16/156688596/what-americans-earn; Brian Stoffel, "Here's How Much the Typical American Made Last Year, By Age and Sex -- How Do You Compare?" *The Motley Fool*, accessed May 1, 2015, http://www.fool.com/investing/general/2015/03/02/heres-how-much-the-typical-american-made-last-ye-2.aspx.

144 A 2002 report from the U.S. Census Bureau showed that throughout the average working life, high school graduates can expect to earn $1.2 million; those with a four-year college degree can expect to earn $2.1 million; those with a master's degree can expect to earn $2.5 million; and those with doctoral and professional degrees earn even more ($3.4 and $4.4 million, respectively). *See* U.S. Census Bureau, "The Big Payoff: Educational Attainment and Synthetic Estimates of Work-Life Earnings," *U.S. Department of Commerce*, accessed April 2, 2015, https://www.census.gov/prod/2002pubs/p23-210.pdf.

- By spending this money, am I acting as if I own it, or am I acting as the Lord's trustee?

- What Scripture requires me to spend this money in this way?

- Can I offer up this purchase as a sacrifice to the Lord?

- Will God reward me for this expenditure at the resurrection of the just?[145]

In other words, if God has entrusted you with a certain amount of His money, and since He also has been gracious enough to allow you to feed and clothe your family with that money, how should you use the amount you have set aside for college? Should you be like the caretaker, spending the Master's money on anything (or any school) the heart desires, or should you use it in a way that advances the goals and desires of the Master (which is really what the believer's heart should desire)? After all, it is His money and "the package doesn't belong to you. You're just the middleman. Your job is to get the package from [God] and deliver it to those [He] want[s] to have it."[146] God's Word is the only place where you can discover where He wants you to invest His money.

Thinking It Through

Some believers never even bother to think about the issue of stewardship as it relates to college choice. They simply choose a college and send tuition checks. These believers have not learned to integrate Scripture with real-life decisions.

Others prayerfully consider the matter and decide that a Bible-believing and Bible-teaching college is the best place for their children to start their independent lives. They send their tuition checks with a sense of purpose.

---

145 Wesley, John. "The Use of Money, Sermon 50." *Wesley Center Online.* Accessed October 5, 2015. http://wesley.nnu.edu/john-wesley/the-sermons-of-john-wesley-1872-edition/sermon-50-the-use-of-money/; Randy Alcorn, *Money, Possessions, and Eternity* (Carol Stream, IL: Tyndale House Publishers, Inc., 1989), 152.
146 Alcorn, *Money, Possessions, and Eternity*, 155.

There is yet another category of believers—those who think about it yet still decide to send their children to a secular college. Some make this decision based on a careful analysis of the character of their children and the school and course of study. They are comfortable in their freedom in Christ to make such a decision (Galatians 5:13) and are expectant that their children will remain centered on Christ throughout the college years, even at that particular school. There may be no sin at all in such a decision and God can be honored with not only the analysis, but also with the result.

However, some from this latter category mistakenly start the analysis by asking this question: "Which is the best school that my child can get into?" And make no mistake—when this is the first question being asked—the "best" typically is judged by secular rankings, meaning the highest ranked school in some secular survey. Sometimes those rankings include categories such as academics, and sometimes they include things like sports, libraries, endowments, faculty, and job placement. Either way, the values most pleasing to God are not on the list. For example, there is no ranking in *U.S. News & World Report* that identifies colleges by their ability to teach the Fruit of the Spirit into their graduates. Likewise, no school ranking survey in *Forbes* elevates issues of the heart and right worship over academic prestige. And there is not a ranking system in *The Princeton Review* that considers whether students are prepared to fulfill the Great Commission upon graduation. Although the absence of any focus on spiritual disciplines should matter to Christians, all too often it does not when colleges are being considered.[147]

Instead of prioritizing increased wisdom over worldly success or prestige, many believers explain their decision to attend secular schools by saying that the goal is to have Christians in all areas and walks of life, which requires some Christians to be on campus at secular colleges. They also conclude that degrees from these respected institutions will allow believing students to obtain the best jobs

---

147 Even rankings of accredited Christian schools mimic the world's judgment by scoring based on the "highest degree of personal attention (student-to-faculty ratio), selectivity (acceptance rate), financial assistance (% receiving financial aid), and student satisfaction (retention and graduation rates)." Michael Templeton, "The 50 Best Christian Colleges in the U.S.," *Christian Universities Online*, accessed August 27, 2015, http://www.christia-nuniversitiesonline.org/best-christian-colleges/.

possible (usually meaning the highest paying jobs), thus affording them the opportunity to hone their God-given talents, influence the world, take care of their families, and give to the church. What could be wrong with that?

Sometimes, there is absolutely nothing wrong with such aspirations, so long as they are God-focused. However, since the human heart is so easily deceived (Jeremiah 17:9; 2 Corinthians 11:3; Ephesians 5:6), believers who venture down this way of thinking should consider whether their assumptions are based in biblical truth. First, believers can and should trust that God is able to provide for His children whether or not they receive a degree from a prestigious university (Matthew 10:31; Luke 11:9-13). It is not necessarily a sin to attend a secular college, but care should be taken to not assume that such a degree is *required* to achieve "success." As discussed above, God measures success differently than the world measures it (Psalm 1:1-3). Second, the "talents" that God is most concerned with are typically not talents that are honed under secular instruction. He desires that His children do justice, love mercy, and walk humbly before Him (Micah 6:8). Such core values and character traits are not featured in many secular college brochures. Third, godly influence in the world is not measured in terms of political persuasion, empire building, or even innovation. While God is present in all such endeavors, the influence He desires is that which was so clearly stated by Jesus before his ascension into heaven: "Go therefore and make disciples of all nations, baptizing them in the name of the Father and of the Son and of the Holy Spirit, teaching them to observe all that I have commanded you" (Matthew 28:19-20).

Again, if the reason for attending a secular institution is to share the good news with non-believing students and to strengthen other believers on campus, then the student's heart may be in the right place; he simply must prepare himself for the battlefield. However, if the argument to attend a secular university is built around the need for a respected résumé in order to influence the world, one should consider the rag-tag group of men that Jesus called to be his disciples. Their lack of formal education did not stop them from influencing the world. A singular commitment to Christ is all that is required (Matthew 5:14-16). Finally, while God can and does use worldly wealth to care for

His children (*see, e.g.,* Exodus 12:35-36). He also can be honored by the widow's penny (Mark 12:41-44).

The point is simply this: God desires that you do all things for His glory (1 Corinthians 10:31). When you consider the issue of stewardship as it relates to your children, your mind, your money, and even your future, are you choosing a college with God's preeminence at the forefront of that decision, or are you putting yourself first? Whether one chooses a secular school or a Christian college, *His* kingdom must be the focus, not yours.

CHAPTER 11

OBJECTIONS AND ANSWERS

One can already hear the objections. "Since my child is already a solid Christian, he certainly can thrive in a non-Christian college and be a light there." Maybe. "My child has a specialized area of study that he wants to pursue, and a small Bible college is probably not going to afford him that opportunity." Perhaps. "My child worked hard in high school and deserves to attend the best university available to him. A Christian college isn't that difficult to get into, so it's not fair to send him to a school he'll feel is beneath him or that won't challenge him intellectually." Wow.

Whether couched in Christian or non-Christian sounding terms, the reasons believers often provide for attending non-Christian colleges are based on anticipated worldly successes that students might attain by attending secular universities.[148] As already discussed, success should be viewed through the eyes of God, not man (Proverbs 29:25). Also, if a student is a Christian, should he seek to build on that Christian foundation for the next four years, or should he be forced to struggle in a place of darkness with fewer believers to lean on? Or does it really matter? After all, life really begins *after* college, right?[149]

---

148 Believers often focus on the freedom available to them (as if it were something other than being freed from the enslavement of sin; Galatians 5:13; Colossians 2:18-23), but they ignore Scripture that appears to disapprove of godless education (Deuteronomy 6:4-9, instructing believers to teach God's commands diligently to children). In fact, since believers are to love God with the entire heart, soul, and mind (Matthew 22:37), then it may follow that if children "are not taught to think like Christians when they study math, history, or science, then they are not obeying the command to love God with all their *minds*." Douglas Wilson, "Scripture Forbids Us to Educate Our Children in the Public Schools," *Center for Reformed Theology and Apologetics,* accessed September 28, 2015, http://www.reformed. org/webfiles/antithesis/index.html?mainframe=/webfiles/antithesis/v2n1/ant_v2n1_issue1. htm.

149 As set forth elsewhere in this book, there are some situations where Christians can attend non-Christian places of learning. Extremely specialized areas of study jump to mind. But this book is about those whose futures are not quite so certain, or whose specialized and technical courses of study are not already set in stone.

To answer that question (whether a college experience really makes much of a difference in a person's walk with the Lord which, if it does, brings the issue of stewardship into play), there are at least three outcomes to consider as a student attends and then graduates from college. Thinking along these lines should provide some clarity of thought for those who seek to rationalize their decision without much regard for real-life outcomes or biblical principles.

First, there is the student who scraps the faith altogether either during, as result of, or after his college experience. He is done with this Christianity thing. He has rejected the faith, he is not a believer, and he is destined for hell without true repentance.

Second, there is the student who pursues his faith vigorously during and after his college experience. He grows and matures into Christ-likeness, taking the process of sanctification very seriously. He is a true believer, intent on building his life with gold, silver, and precious stones, looking forward to the day when he is rewarded for his faithful service by the grace of God (1 Corinthians 3:12-15).

Third, there is the student who halfheartedly pursues his faith during and after college. He has one foot in the world and one foot in the church. Upon graduation, he attends church on most Sundays but never really gets involved; he sometimes reads his Bible and sporadically participates in Bible studies through his church. He rarely incorporates a biblical worldview into his work life and fails to see the urgency in evangelism. His life, once established with family, is quickly enveloped by kids, sports, work, and debt. He never is satisfied completely because his commitment to pursue Christ is weak and easily sidetracked. He often is frustrated because he knows that when he does open the Bible, it speaks directly to his situation, but he does not follow it with his whole heart, nor is he diligent in his study of the Word. He lives a defeated Christian life since it is built with hay, straw, and stubble, having very little everlasting value (1 Corinthians 3:12-15). He then raises children who observe a parent who does not cling to God (Psalm 63:8). These children often make the same college choice that he did. The cycle repeats.

As seen from each of these three scenarios, the college years *can* have an impact on a person's spiritual life (just like grade school and high school can have such an impact). In fact, *every* moment in a person's life can have lasting value and God will use every moment for His purpose (Romans 8:28). There is no period of time that believers should disregard or write off as unredeemed or neutral. Humans are either for God or against Him (Matthew 12:30). As such, believers should be wholeheartedly *for* Him during the college years. This leads back to the discussion of stewardship.

If God were to ask His children how they manage the money He gives them for college, or how believers work through the college choice decision-making process, or how they intend to spend the four college years, what would the response be? If none of that money is spent on an education or experience that fosters a delight in God's Word, if there is no diligent study of God's plan and how it relates to college choice, and if the four years spent in college are, at best, spiritually neutral, shouldn't that provoke a sense of shame? At the judgment, will these stewards of God's resources stare at the ground while that part of life burns up as if it were hay, straw, and stubble? On the other hand, if the goal is to please Him and a careful, biblical analysis is undertaken to arrive at a spiritually sound decision to invest in an educational experience that glorifies God, Christians can look forward to hearing the Creator say, "Well done, good and faithful servant" (Matthew 25:23). The idea is not to somehow obtain salvation by works, but rather, to demonstrate a love for God by proving to be a faithful steward in *all* decisions, including those that relate to the college choice.[150]

Although there likely are some Christian students and situations that call for entry into secular schools, the biblical principles set forth herein seem to indicate that the majority of believing students should spend their time on Christian campuses if they have that option. Some, however, still raise objections to this strong stance against a secular education, even when the discussion revolves solely around faith issues (as opposed to other practical reasons, such as the cost of

---

150 In reality, non-Christian education is not neutral. "[A] presumed neutrality toward academic study is really a secularism that oppresses Christian students. God is left out...." John White, "Secular Enslavement," in *What Does the Lord Require of You?* ed. Lynn R. Buzzard (Beaver Falls, Pennsylvania: Geneva School of Law, 1997), 83.

college, location, or specialized fields of study, which are addressed elsewhere in this book). These objections often stem from the argument that Christians should not be so isolated from the world that they fail to influence it. According to this way of thinking, Christians should not have a fortress mentality. The proponents of this position cite the oft-quoted saying that believers should be "in the world but not of the world." Their argument is divided into two parts. First, Christians only can impact the world for Christ by participating in it (or at least understanding it through personal experience).[151] Second, Christians only can grow in their faith by being tested by the non-Christian world. Put another way, proponents of this position argue that true faith will stand the tests thrown at it by the world and will emerge deeper and stronger, while at the same time influencing others for the gospel.[152] Each of these points is addressed in the following.

Is Exposure the Key to Influence?

The first point—that a Christian needs to be in the world to impact it—directs the believer to become a "student of culture," and a secular college is a good place to do so since it is a blend of many different views, races, religions, and politics. It is assumed that only by being exposed to these differences in a secular college will a student really understand and be able to influence the world for Christ.

> Being at college is like being at a giant, non-stop sleepover. Maybe this is a frightening image but I mean to only convey the closeness which you find between yourself and new friends. Many of your friends will

---

151 This should not be construed as personal participation in sin; rather, the argument is for exposure to how others live, think, feel, and act, in order to influence them for Christ. As one Christian leader put it, "Dartmouth is never going to become [a purposefully Christian college] again. I'm not going to reclaim the Ivy League. In some ways, I appreciate the contrast. It's like diamonds on black velvet, the Christians who are here in the midst of this environment." Collin Hansen, "The Holy and the Ivy," *Christianity Today*, accessed April 13, 2015, http://www.christianitytoday.com/ct/2005/september/26.64.html?start=5.

152 *See, e.g.*, Christopher Unseth, "3 Reasons Christians Should Consider a Non-Christian College," *Relevant Magazine*, accessed April 15, 2015, http://www.relevantmag-azine.com/relevant-u/undergrad/3-reasons-christians-should-attend-non-christian-college#comments; KC McGinnis, "6 Ways to Waste Your College Education," *Relevant Magazine*, accessed April 15, 2015, http://www.relevantmagazine.com/relevant-u/undergrad/6-ways-waste-your-college-education.

have never read the Bible or even met a "normal" person who calls him or herself a Christian. Your dorm is the starting line for several years of intense friendship forging and within these new relationships, your walk with God will reverberate throughout the lives of your friends.[153]

While it is correct to describe the secular college experience as one that offers exposure to various aspects of humanity, it is incorrect (and unbiblical) to assume that exposure to godless or morally reprehensible teaching or influence is necessary to be used by God as instruments of His righteousness and influence. In fact, the thinking that gives rise to the above quote appears contrary to Scripture to the extent that "intense friendship forging" unequally yokes believers with non-believers (2 Corinthians 6:14) or exposes believers to the consistent influence of sinners (Psalm 1:1-3).[154] Further, the saying that believers are to be "in the world but not of the world" is simply a misquote of Scripture that paints a much starker contrast:

> If you were of the world, the world would love you as its own; but because you are not of the world, but I chose you out of the world, therefore the world hates you. (John 15:19)

In his high priestly prayer to the Father, Jesus says the following about sanctification and being in the world:

> I have given them your word, and the world has hated them because they are not of the world, just as I am not of the world. I do not ask that you take them out of the world, but that you keep them from the evil one. They are not of the world, just as I am not of the world. Sanctify them in the truth; your word is truth. As you sent me into the world, so I have sent them into the world. And for their sake I consecrate myself, that they

---

153 Unseth, "3 Reasons Christians Should Consider a Non-Christian College."
154 The metaphor of unequal yoking would have been understood by New Testament Christians who knew the folly of tying two different types of beasts together (the ox and the ass) that have different demeanors and strengths.

also may be sanctified in truth. (John 17:14-19)

While the argument sometimes is made that Jesus sent his disciples "into the world" and, therefore, his followers should do the same in a secular college, Jesus' words should not be taken out of context. He prayed that his followers would be sanctified in the truth—God's Word. While not impossible for a college student to learn God's Word through some independent study, church attendance, and other fellowship, it is difficult to imagine a secular school experience providing the same level of immersion into God's Word—and with the same goal—as a Christian college.[155]

Further, there is very little biblical support for the proposition that being exposed to worldly thinking increases God's influence. Most every believer has heard the argument. "Well, Jesus didn't avoid sinners. In fact, he spent time with them. We should, too. For their sake, of course." But Jesus made it clear that he was there to influence, not to be influenced. He was not sitting at the feet of sinners to learn, he was not trying to understand where they were coming from, and he was not intent on forging deep friendships with non-believers. Likewise, although Paul understood the pagan religions and used that information when preaching the good news to the philosophers in Athens, there is nothing to suggest that as a believer he spent significant time voluntarily exposing himself to pagan thought in order to be more influential (Acts 17). In fact, he even warned believers to be on guard that "no one takes you captive by philosophy and empty deceit, according to human tradition" (Colossians 2:8). His warning

---

155 This argument is sometimes framed in the following way: "Expand your horizons." Of course, this is just another way of telling believers that they should expose themselves to other ways of thinking. Not only can a Christian college provide such other viewpoints (and how they vary from Scripture), but such a statement minimizes the dangers of a confused, watered-down believer who has lost his saltiness (Luke 14:34). It also ignores the risks associated with a secular college (whether social or curriculum based), and it demeans the riches found in an infinite God. While there is nothing inherently wrong with trying to understand secular thinking in order to more effectively present the gospel, it should always be remembered that those who ascribe to and are taken captive with that way of thinking are lost in their darkened minds (Romans 1:21; 1 Corinthians 1:20, 27; 1 Corinthians 3:19; Ephesians 4:18). As it has been said, one can keep an open mind, "but not so open that your brains fall out." Garson O'Toole, "Do not be so open-minded that your brains fall out," *Quote Investigator*, accessed September 25, 2015, http://quoteinvestigator.com/2014/04/13/open-mind/.

was not ill-founded. He knew that exposure to worldly thinking has the potential to ensnare (Acts 20:29-31; 2 Timothy 2:26; Psalm 141:9). And even if a believer is not completely sold on the supposed "truth" that the pagans offer, he can be lured by what is perceived as the easier or more enjoyable lifestyle they flaunt. Even Asaph, the inspired author of a number of holy psalms, found this temptation almost too much to bear.

> But as for me, my feet had almost stumbled,
>   My steps had nearly slipped.
> For I was envious of the arrogant
>   When I saw the prosperity of the wicked.
> For they have no pangs until death;
>   Their bodies are fat and sleek.
> They are not in trouble as others are;
>   They are not stricken like the rest of mankind.
> Therefore pride is their necklace;
>   Violence covers them as a garment.
> Their eyes swell out through fatness;
>   Their hearts overflow with follies.
> They scoff and speak with malice;
>   Loftily they threaten oppression.
> They set their mouths against the heavens,
>   And their tongue struts through the earth...
> Behold, these are the wicked;
>   Always at ease, they increase in riches.
> All in vain have I kept my heart clean
>   And washed my hands in innocence. (Psalm 73:2-9, 12-13)

Only when he sought God's wisdom was Asaph able to escape the trap that had been so neatly set.

> But when I thought how to understand this,
>   It seemed to me a wearisome task,
> Until I went into the sanctuary of God;
>   Then I discerned their end.
> Truly you set them in slippery places;
>   You make them fall to ruin.
> How they are destroyed in a moment,

Swept away utterly by terrors! (Psalm 73:16-19)

Likewise, when Jesus sent his disciples into the world to "make disciples" and to teach them "to observe all that I have commanded" (Matthew 28:19-20), he was affirming the source of real influence—the Word of God. Seeking to fit in, to understand, or to be exposed to other cultures, beliefs, or experiences has nothing to do with it. God's Word alone will accomplish His purpose (Isaiah 55:11). His children are not required to test their faith or pursue others by visiting dens of iniquity for extended periods of time (*see also* Proverbs 22:3; 27:12).

So what about that rare student who is spiritually mature, biblically trained, and intent on impacting the secular campus for Christ? He takes his role as salt and light very seriously (Matthew 5:13-16). As indicated above, there is not a biblically precise answer for every single person on the issue of college choice. However, great care should be taken to ensure that the salt does not lose its saltiness, and that the light does not fail to shine. "My son, if sinners entice you, do not consent" (Proverbs 1:10). Thinking oneself to be beyond the contagion of sin is foolish, and pride often comes before the fall (1 Corinthians 10:12). As one author put it:

> I do not dismiss the argument that Christian young people have the opportunity to be salt and light at non-Christian colleges. Unfortunately, however, the reality does not live up to this vision, admirable though it is. Research plainly shows that most students are unprepared for the conflict of worldviews they will encounter at non-Christian colleges and universities. Dropping a beautiful diamond into the mud will not purify the mud. Rather it may dirty the gem until it is unrecognizable.[156]

Finally, some argue that exposure to a secular college is the key to influence in the post-graduate secular world—for the glory of God, of course. This argument is sometimes couched in language that makes it seem as if Christians should attend high-ranking secular colleges

---

156 Henderson, "Investing in Their Faith."

to be intellectually challenged and to secure more esteemed positions in order to influence the world. According to this way of thinking, Christian colleges do not have the resources, faculty, or student body to challenge high-achieving students and so high-achieving believers should build their résumés elsewhere in order to land the best jobs. Doing so will later allow them to work in positions of influence. Such an argument not only ignores the high quality of education provided by a number of Christian colleges, but more importantly it ignores the hand of God in all things, including job prospects and influence (Proverbs 16:9). A believer starting down this way of thinking should analyze his own heart to be sure that it is God's glory he is seeking, as opposed to the fulfillment of his own selfish ambitions (Philippians 2:3).

Is Exposure the Key to Stronger Faith?

The second point that argues against the perceived isolation that accompanies a Christian education tends to equate spiritual growth with exposure to temptation, trials, and challenges, especially to one's faith. Consider these statements.

- "Coming out of college, you will be thankful to have met adversity with a willingness to learn about your own positions and the positions of others. If you are truly in love with the truth of Christ, then objections to your faith by others will only result in you developing a deeper understanding of it."[157]

- "During your four years or more in academia, you will probably challenge the intellectual foundations of your long-held beliefs, and you may even have doubts. *This is a good thing.* In fact, a crisis of faith in early adulthood is probably the best thing for your faith. Earnest soul searching leads to a deeper, more genuine faith."[158]

- "The secular culture often acts as a test...The faith that comes out is purified."[159]

---

157 Unseth, "3 Reasons Christians Should Consider a Non-Christian College."

158 McGinnis, "6 Ways to Waste Your College Education."

159 John Fortenbury, "The Christian Decision: Attend a Christian or Secular College?"

As for the general proposition—that testing and trials produce a persevering faith—even Scripture agrees (James 1:2-4, "Count it all joy, my brothers, when you meet trials of various kinds, for you know that the testing of your faith produces steadfastness. And let steadfastness have its full effect, that you may be perfect and complete, lacking in nothing"). However, there is nothing to support the more specific proposition that believers should go looking for trials or temptations. The world—and every person's heart—is full of enough darkness to put the Christian faith to the test without being required to sit through four years of constant institutional and social testing. Indeed, the writer of Proverbs advises that, "The prudent sees danger and hides himself, but the simple go on and suffer for it" (Proverbs 22:3; 27:12). Simply put, shielding oneself from certain situations and teachings might be the wisest course of action, as opposed to voluntarily paying for that experience. Further, the Bible says that faith comes through hearing the Word of Christ (Romans 10:17). If one were to listen for the Word of God at most secular college campuses, not much would be heard. Faith is not designed to grow in the absence of God's Word, so expecting faith to increase in that setting (when compared to a school where Scripture is taught and contemplated every day) is contrary to God's teaching.

Sometimes, however, those advocating for such exposure take a different route and do not necessarily focus on temptations or attacks. As one writer put it,

> We've all heard it: College is a "dark place." It's full of liberals, postmoderns, party-goers, religious fanatics, environmentalists and other "dangers" to your faith. You've been told to avoid these people, hole up in a nice Christian community and work on that law degree. This is your only hope for escaping higher education. But it needn't be so. College is a blend of cultures, races, religions and political views. You're going to meet more people who are different from you than who are like you. You might even become friends with

---

USA Today, accessed April 15, 2015, http://college.usatoday.com/2012/09/13/the-christian-decision-attend-a-christian-or-secular-college/.

these people. And you will be better for it.[160]

At first blush, that line of thinking makes sense. It appeals to our sensibilities to be kind to non-believers and to enjoy our freedom in Christ. However, it goes too far to conclude that exposure to the world will make believers "better." Scripture repeatedly warns of such exposure and cautions believers to be on guard against becoming like those who practice evil (Galatians 5:13; Psalm 1:1; 1 Corinthians 15:33). Indeed, God's children will be at their best (meaning, in a glorified state) once they are in heaven, where no unbelief exists (1 Corinthians 13:12; 1 John 3:2). It is not exposure to different people and ways of thinking that makes one "better." It is constant exposure and adherence to God's Word, and reliance on the promise that He will conform His children to the image of Christ (Romans 8:29; Hebrews 5:12-14).

None of this is to say that Christians should be complete isolationists or avoid all interactions with the world. That, too, would be contrary to Scripture (*see* Matthew 28:29-20). The question is whether the Christian faith *needs* exposure to diverse thinking (meaning secular thinking, teaching, and influence) during the college years in order to grow. Framed differently, is such exposure *required* to root out false assurances of salvation and to identify true believers? The answer, of course, is "no." God's Word, as evidenced by the Fruit of the Spirit in the lives of true believers, is what does that (Matthew 7:17-22; Galatians 5:22-23). As one writer stated,

> [The Christian faith] is a critical element woven into the fabric of the [Christian] college experience. The Christian dynamic is evident not just in chapel or a Sunday service, but also during pizza in the dorm at midnight, during an honest debate over moral and theological principles in the dining hall, and during a discussion of ethics in regards to career and family. The Christian component is noticeable in the classroom, but it is not limited by those walls. I believe this is the real difference of a Christian college environment, as well as a key reason why there has been such tremendous

160 McGinnis, "6 Ways to Waste Your College Education."

growth at Christian colleges ... Such campuses should not be viewed as an opportunity to avoid the world, but rather as an opportunity to **influence** the world. The years spent within a Christian college environment can aid the student's ability to serve, thrive, and become a modern day follower of Jesus Christ—regardless of their profession. Christian colleges are in a unique position to honestly address the spiritual and moral issues that people of every age face every day. People can spend years in training for their chosen profession, sport, and hobbies. Christian colleges can offer all of those opportunities, but within a Christian context where the student becomes more prepared to impact and live within our world.[161]

Knowing that attending a secular college is not required for faith to grow—and understanding that it could be harmful—should lead all believers to consider carefully the options available. As Paul phrased it, although all things are permissible, not all things are beneficial (1 Corinthians 6:12; 10:23). God's children should select the college that is *most* beneficial to their faith, to the glory of God. Don't settle for second best. Instead, seek God's glory in all things, knowing that "your faith is not necessarily going to thrive at a Christian or non-Christian college, it will thrive only if you decide to make it a priority in your life."[162]

---

161 Thom Seagren, "Christian Colleges v. Secular Colleges: What's the Difference?" *The Christian Connector, Inc.*, accessed April 15, 2015, http://www.christianconnector.com/Christian-college-tips/Selecting-Best-College-Christian-vs-Secular.cfm.

162 Unseth, "3 Reasons Christians Should Consider a Non-Christian College."

CHAPTER 12

ONE SIZE DOES NOT FIT ALL
(BUT BE CAREFUL!)

Ok, ok. So the right choice for most believers is to pursue a Christian college experience that elevates Scripture and right living for the glory of God. But is that the *only* choice that can please God? The short answer is "probably not," but care should be taken when venturing into the world for an education.[163]

To begin with, one can imagine a scenario where a Christian college does not fulfill a specific vocational calling of a college-bound student. However, this is not meant to provide a justification or rationalization for avoiding a Christian education. If pressed, everyone probably could come up with an argument as to why a secular school would be better suited for the student's particular "calling." This type of self-serving reasoning might look like this:

- "I really want to work on Wall Street, so in order to get into a reputable MBA program, I need to be at a top four-year university."

- "I am going to be a doctor, so I need to be at the best Ivy League school to prepare my résumé for medical school applications."

- "I expect to teach Spanish someday, and I've heard that the foreign languages department at the University of So-and-So is the best."

- "To serve God as a lawyer someday, I will only go so far with a Christian college on my résumé. I need to go somewhere that law firm recruiters will respect."

---

163 It should be noted that there are some who believe that secular education is a sin. *See* David d'Escoto, "Is it a Sin to Send Our Kids to Public School?" *WND Commentary*, accessed April 15, 2015, http://www.wnd.com/2009/06/102269/#!

- "I'm not going into full-time Christian ministry, so I don't need to go to a Christian college with so much Bible emphasis."

This type of reasoning has some logic. After all, Christian colleges—for the most part—are *not* as known or respected by the world (including graduate schools and employers) as schools like Harvard, Northwestern, University of Texas, or UCLA. Again, however, the question must be asked: Who is your audience? Is the goal to get into the best graduate program and to be hired for the best job (in the world's eyes)? Or is the goal to pursue excellence on God's terms, possibly being willing to forego some of those supposedly better opportunities in exchange for an education that will align your thinking more and more with God's plan for your life?[164]

That being said, every child of God—though part of the Body of Christ and with a specific role to fulfill—is distinct. There are some believing students who have a God-given, laser-beam focus on a particular vocation that might not be offered at a standard Christian college (or even a standard secular school). Examples might include flight training, a specialized underwater welding program, a dance or arts or military academy, or a specific architectural program. These are exceptions, however, and a decision to forego a Christian education in favor of such a secular program should not be made without much prayer, meditation, study, and consultation with mature believers.[165] In short, care should be taken to not be conformed to the world (Romans 12:2).

John Bunyan's (1628-1688) classic work, *The Pilgrim's Progress,* provides an illustration of the dangers associated with passing through such a worldly (and tempting) place. In the story, the main character (Christian) travels with his companion (Faithful) on the straight

---

164 The idea that an education at a Christian college will limit a student's post-graduate options is unsupported. However, even this line of thinking raises the question, "Is the goal a successful life according to worldly standards, or an eternally significant life?"

165 As one opponent of secular education said, "[My children] are being trained to hold and apply a Christian worldview. I am not trying to keep them from encounters with those who hate God; I am trying to train them and prepare them for it." Douglas Wilson, "Scripture Forbids Us to Educate Our Children in the Public Schools," *Center for Reformed Theology and Apologetics,* accessed September 28, 2015, http://www.reformed.org/webfiles/antithesis/index.html?mainframe=/webfiles/antithesis/v2n1/ant_v2n1_issue1.htm.

and narrow King's highway toward the Celestial City. This narrow path, however, leads straight through the worldly town called Vanity Fair. The town's residents offer all kinds of tempting things for sale, including material possessions, real estate, and positions of honor, titles, husbands, wives, children, precious stones, and even souls. In other words, there is something for everyone, with some blatantly evil items and some that seem relatively harmless. However, when Christian and Faithful pass through the town, they can only ward off the solicitations of the salespeople by sticking their fingers in their ears and crying to themselves to turn their eyes away from vanity. When pressed, they state that they will buy only truth.

The steadfast position of the travelers results in a loud cry and commotion from the townspeople. Christian and Faithful are mocked, beaten, thrown into jail, and Faithful is ultimately burned at the stake for his position. Only through supernatural intervention does Christian continue on his journey.[166]

The application to college choice should be obvious. For the serious Christian, passing time in this world will include many temptations to sin, and will result in persecution, especially if non-conformity is the standard. Of course, there are some 18-year-old high school students who are more mature in their Christian walk than some 81-year-old pew sitters. Perhaps they are more able to withstand the temptations and associations that exist in secular schools than less mature believers (*see* Daniel 1, for example, which discusses faithful Jewish teenagers who remained faithful despite a godless education). Further, there are some secular schools with extremely strong Christian clubs on campus and these organizations provide fantastic opportunities for growth, evangelism, and outreach.[167] However, none of these factors

---

166 John Bunyan, *The Pilgrim's Progress (in Today's English)*, retold by James Thomas (Chicago, IL: Moody Publishers, 1992), 87-98.

167 Remember, however, that "an organization and a name do not make a church. One hundred religious persons knit into a unity by careful organization do not constitute a church any more than eleven dead men make a football team." A.W. Tozer, *Man: The Dwelling Place of God*, in *Gems from Tozer* (Harrisburg, PA: Christian Publications, Inc., 1969), 48. While there is no denying that there are solid Christian organizations on certain campuses that provide some sense of community, fellowship, and growth, these groups are no substitute for consistent involvement in a local church. *But see* Collin Hansen, "The Holy and the Ivy," *Christianity Today*, accessed April 13, 2015, http://www.christianitytoday.com/ct/2005/september/26.64.html?start=5 (discussing Christian faith and organizations at Ivy

should muddle the clear dangers associated with being immersed in a fully secular school whose goal is to influence students toward worldly thinking. Indeed, "bad company ruins good morals" (1 Corinthians 15:33; *see also* Proverbs 13:20; 22:3; 27:12). Sin is in the business of destruction—and business is booming (Proverbs 27:20). Therefore, be wise. Be an influencer for good. Do not associate with evil or be swayed by its pleasures. "Do not be conformed to this world, but be transformed by the renewal of your mind, that by testing you may discern what is the will of God, what is good and acceptable and perfect" (Romans 12:2).

League schools).

CHAPTER 13

WHAT TO LOOK FOR IN A CHRISTIAN COLLEGE

According to the world, a good friend is someone who wants the best for you, who is honest with you, and who is a good influence on you.[168] The "best," of course, is God's plan which is set forth in the Bible; "honesty" requires truth, which is found only in God's Word; and "good" influences are rooted in Scripture. In short, "he is your friend who pushes you nearer to God,"[169] and that comes only from the application of God's Word to one's life. A college should be held to this same standard and should act as a good friend in terms of desiring the best for you, conveying truth to you, and being a good influence on you, all as measured by Scripture.

God's children are commanded to "grow in the grace and knowledge of our Lord and Savior Jesus Christ" (2 Peter 3:18). The only way to experience such growth is through study and application of Scripture. Through the Bible, God has provided everything His children need to live a godly life, through the knowledge of Christ (2 Peter 1:3). In fact, heavy criticism is levied upon those who stagnate in their faith, who have not diligently trained themselves through Scripture, and who remain spiritually immature (Hebrews 5:12-14; 1 Peter 2:2-3).[170] When considering these precepts in terms of college choice, it is fairly easy to see that a typical secular school will not, as an institution, present God's Word as truth, nor will it push students to grow in the Christian faith. A secular school often is *not* a "good friend" to the believer.[171]

---

168 *Urban Dictionary,* s.v. "Good Friend," accessed August 26, 2015, http://www.urban-dictionary.com/define.php?term=Good+Friend; Alex Lickerman, "The True Meaning of Friendship," *Psychology Today,* accessed August 26, 2015, https://www.psychologytoday.com/blog/happiness-in-world/201312/the-true-meaning-friendship.

169 Abraham Kuyper, "Abraham Kuyper Quotes," *Good Reads,* accessed October 6, 2015, http://www.goodreads.com/quotes/17308-he-is-your-friend-who-pushes-you-nearer-to-god.

170 Got Questions Ministries, "What does it mean for a Christian to grow in the faith?" *GotQuestions.org,* accessed April 17, 2015, http://www.gotquestions.org/Christian-grow-faith.html.

171 Of the thousands of secular colleges that exist, not all are equally hostile to God's

Applying the same logic, however, it is clear that not all Christian schools and Christian college experiences are created equal. Adherence to and respect for God's Word will vary from school to school, and just having the name "Christian" associated with a college does not make it so. Further, even a "Christian" education can be a waste if it does not prepare students to confront the attacks on their worldview that surely will come as soon as they graduate from college.[172] Accordingly, the student who wants to please God and grow in his faith must ask the following question: If the constant study and use of God's Word will increase discernment and spiritual growth, how much of that will I receive at a particular Christian college?[173] The answer varies depending on the school, and because the choice one makes for college will shape much of that student's life, a student choosing among various "Christian" schools should consider the following.

A Christian College Should Encourage Students to Know God

If "what comes into our minds when we think about God is the most important thing about us,"[174] then we should make every effort to ensure that what we think about God is 100% true and that we have as much accurate information about Him as possible. Such an endeavor can *only* take place in a setting where God's people are combing through Scripture together, being led by more mature believers, and applying the light to their lives on a daily basis. Truth-finding *cannot* be optimized in a setting where God is mocked, the Bible is reduced to a book of myths, or where spiritual growth is an afterthought that might be crammed into the few extra moments one might find in a

---

Word. Some, in fact, promote Judeo-Christian values and share many of the same views as Christians on a variety of social, economic, and political issues. While such schools may be easier for a Christian to attend and maintain his Christian values, it must be recognized that "good works" or "good values" are insufficient to save. The gospel of Jesus Christ is *the* truth that leads to life. Apart from him, there is no other (Acts 4:12).

172 Phillip Johnson, foreword to *Total Truth*, by Nancy Pearcey, 12.

173 "The true measure of spiritual growth is not how much knowledge you've gained in the past year, but how much you've grown in holiness." Tim Challies, "Sanctification is a Community Project," citing Mike Bullmore, *Challies.Com*, accessed October 6, 2015, http://www.challies.com/christian-living/sanctification-is-a-community-project.

174 A.W. Tozer, *The Knowledge of the Holy* (New York: HarperCollins Publishers Inc., 1961), 1.

week filled with secular studies and activities. In short, a Christian college should be a place where God is

- Sought (Jeremiah 29:13; Matthew 6:33),

- Praised (Psalm 35:18; 1 Peter 2:9), and

- Acknowledged as the Creator of the universe (Psalm 104; Nehemiah 9:6; Romans 11:36; Revelation 4:11).

If a college is not encouraging students to know God in this way, then it is not an institution with biblical priorities.

A Christian College Should Teach Students to Pursue Righteousness

When analyzing Christian colleges, students should consider the words of Jesus: "Whoever has my commandments and keeps them, he it is who loves me. And he who loves me will be loved by my Father, and I will love him and manifest myself to him" (John 14:21). To make it even clearer, Jesus continued, "If anyone loves me, he will keep my word, and my Father will love him, and we will come to him and make our home with him. Whoever does not love me does not keep my words" (John 14:23-24). God values a right heart and obedience, which is how His children demonstrate love for Him.

A Christian college worthy of attendance is one that will encourage students to obey God in all things. "Whatever man may stand, whatever he may do, to whatever he may apply his hand—in agriculture, in commerce, and in industry, or his mind, in the world of art, and science—he is, in whatsoever it may be, constantly standing before the face of God. He is employed in the service of his God. He has strictly obeyed his God. And above all, he has to aim at the glory of his God."[175]

---

175 Abraham Kuyper, "Abraham Kuyper Quotes," *Good Reads,* accessed October 7, 2015, https://www.goodreads.com/quotes/843713-whatever-man-may-stand-whatever-he-may-do-to-whatever.

A school dedicated to righteous living will cultivate a love for God's law in the heart of its students. In other words, they should grow in their love for God's standard and long for the righteousness that God's plan provides.[176] Serving God by seeking His glory and obeying His commands should start with the fulfillment of the Great Commission, which includes the command to go and make more disciples who will obey his commands (Matthew 28:19-20). After all, Jesus is "the way, and the truth, and the life" (John 14:6), and he said that "the harvest is plentiful, but the laborers are few" (Luke 10:2). If a school does not instruct its students to fulfill the command to evangelize and make disciples, it is unlikely to be one that is pursuing what God values.[177]

A Christian College Should Equip Believers and Not Be a Waste of Time

For those who think of the college years as just something to get through—with little regard for spiritual things—A.J. Tozer's words should ring in their ears: "Time is a resource that is non-renewable and nontransferable. You cannot store it, slow it up, hold it up, divide it up or give it up. You can't hoard it up or save it for a rainy day—when it's lost it is unrecoverable. When you kill time, remember that it has no resurrection."[178] Do not merely pass through this life. Redeem every moment, including your college years, as if it were your last and you were preparing a gift for the Father as you look forward to seeing Him face to face for the very first time.

In order to prepare such a gift, it is important to know the truth so that you can arrange life accordingly. In fact, the truth is the only thing that can free people from the bondage of sin (John 8:32). For this reason, God intends that some act as teachers, evangelists, and shepherds "to equip the saints" in order to build up the Body of Christ (Ephesians 4:11-12). In this way, the Body of believers is built up in love as its

---

176 Douglas Wilson, *Standing on the Promises* (Moscow, ID: Canon Press, 1997); Douglas Wilson, "Parenting Young People I," *Blog and Mablog,* accessed October 7, 2015, http://dougwils.com/s8-expository/parenting-young-people-i.html.

177 *See* Daniel 12:3 ("And those who are wise shall shine like the brightness of the sky above; and those who turn many to righteousness, like the stars forever and ever.").

178 A.W. Tozer, *The Pursuit of God* (Camp Hill, PA: Christian Publications, Inc., 1982).

grows (Ephesians 4:16). As such, a Christian college should equip students with the truth and should foster a love for that truth in order to proclaim it, all with the goal of building up the Body of Christ.[179]

Likewise, a Christian college should equip believers to stand firm against dark opposition to the faith. Although parents should be intimately involved in the training of their children, there are often gaps in that training. John Milton (1608-1674) perhaps stated it best when he spoke of the influence that imperfect parents have on their children, and the goal of education to remedy some of those shortcomings: "The end then of learning is to repair the ruins of our first parents by regaining to know God aright, and out of that knowledge to love him, to imitate him, to be like him, as we may the nearest by possessing our souls of true virtue, which being united to the heavenly grace of faith makes up the highest perfection."[180]

The shortcomings of Christian parents to prepare their children to understand the world and the seriousness of their faith are even more evident today. For example, in colonial times, church membership required candidates to learn the Bible, the Lord's Prayer, church creeds, the Ten Commandments, and the catechism, all of which was followed by a rigorous examination by church elders and a credible conversion testimony.[181] However, sometime during the Great Awakening, many sermons devolved from instructional to emotional conversion experiences.[182] Instead of struggle, study, and complete surrender as evidenced by a moral lifestyle, all that was needed was a crisis of conversion; revivalist preachers offered assurance of salvation on the spot.[183] While there is biblical support for such a moment of salvation, the lack of emphasis in the lives of these "converts" on Bible study and righteous living started some American churches on a descent into an anti-intellectual framework for Christianity. In some denominations,

---

179 MacArthur, "John MacArthur on Choosing a College."

180 John Milton, *Tractate on Education*, Vol. III, Part 4, in *The Harvard Classics* (New York: P.F. Collier & Son, 1909-1914), accessed September 17, 2015, http://www.bartleby.com/3/4/1.html.

181 Patricia Bonomi, *Under the Cope of Heaven: Religion, Society, and Politics in Colonial America* (New York: Oxford University Press, 1986), 158-159.

182 Pearcey, *Total Truth*, 263.

183 Ibid., 278.

this pattern has continued to the present day, and many parents who are now ill-equipped themselves simply have not prepared their children to be released into an unbelieving world with any apologetic tools to guard against powerful and intelligent sounding authority figures (professors) who might attempt to undermine their faith.[184]

In light of these two truths—that believers are called to minister to one another, and that the world will send consistent and vigorous attacks on God's children—a worthy Christian college will make a priority the equipping of its students in the way of the Lord.[185]

A Christian College Should Teach Students How and Why the Bible Is the Supreme Authority for Godly Living

In Brazilian jiu-jitsu, there is a common mantra: "Position before submission." The idea is that before a fighter can make his opponent submit (surrender), he must first gain control by being in the correct position. Such thinking also translates into the Christian life. Before a person will submit to biblical counsel, God's Word must first be in

---

184 This is not to say that all believers in the 18th and 19th centuries were anti-intellectual—far from it. In fact, there were many who went to the other extreme, rejecting what they perceived as an emotional movement, and instead developing a fortress mentality which somewhat isolated them from the world, including academia. Pearcey, *Total Truth*, 291. There was a division of labor, where churches withdrew from intellectual encounters with the secular world and abandoned the sciences and rational studies. Ibid., 323. As de Tocqueville noted from his travels to the United States during that time, "The American clergy stand aloof from secular affairs," and "in America, religion is a distinct sphere, in which the priest is sovereign but out of which he takes care never to go." Alexis de Tocqueville, *Democracy in America*, vol. 2 (New York: J. & H. G. Langley, 1840), 27. Without the presence of strong Christian voices in education—and in light of this new separation of intellect and spirituality—humanistic thinking grew and many Christians were not only uninvolved in the system, but they were then unprepared to combat it once it had taken hold.

185 For those who question whether the world is truly hostile to the Christian faith, *see* Daniel Dennett, *Darwin's Dangerous Idea* (New York: Simon & Schuster 1995), 63; *see also* Nick Humphrey, "What Shall We Tell the Children?" Amnesty Lecture, Oxford, February 21, 1997, accessed September 17, 2015, https://www.youtube.com/watch?v=y-fr6SkaBuq0 (8:00 minute mark) ("Children have a right not to have their minds addled by nonsense. And we as a society have a duty to protect them from it. So we should no more allow parents to teach their children to believe, for example, in the literal truth of the Bible . . . than we should allow parents to knock their children's teeth out or lock them in a dungeon").

the correct position in that person's life. Until Scripture is elevated to its rightful place in an individual's life as the supreme source of godly wisdom, the individual will never surrender to it.

Most schools that call themselves "Christian" at least pay lip service to their religious heritage or to the Bible. In fact, many have Christian-sounding mission statements that easily can confuse prospective students who might not know to dig deeper. Even a brief sampling of these schools' websites, however, demonstrates a fundamental contradiction between scriptural precepts and the values actually honored by some of these institutions. For example, one calls itself "unambiguously Christian," yet touts over 30 different on-campus religious beliefs. This school brags that some of its students are atheists, Mormons, Jehovah's Witnesses, Hindus, Buddhists, and Muslims, as well as the fact that students are not required to embrace Christianity.[186] Others talk about chapel and spiritual life, but also advertise homosexual student organizations. Not surprisingly, most of these colleges employ faculty with incredibly divergent beliefs on the accuracy or meaning of the Bible. Some believe it is God's Word, others think that portions can be carved out, while still others view Scripture more as a general guideline. In short, when deciding among Christian colleges, a student should consider whether or not the institution elevates Scripture to its rightful place, or whether the school's supposed commitment to biblical teaching is just superficial lip service. If a school has decided that appealing to the masses is more important than adhering to God's Word, it is not a school that is pleasing God and certainly will not cultivate a love for His Word during the college years. In fact, "God hates those who misrepresent his Word or speak lies in His name,"[187] so a college that is "Christian" in name only is one to be avoided. God hates hypocrisy, "You hypocrites! Well did Isaiah prophesy of you, when he said: 'This people honors me with their lips, but their heart is far from me; in vain do they worship me, teaching as doctrines the commandments of men'" (Matthew 15:7-9; Revelation 3:16).

Against that backdrop, prospective students and their parents should

---

186 Baylor University, "Christian Commitment," *Baylor.edu*, accessed August 27, 2015, http://www.baylor.edu/about/index.php?id=88782.

187 MacArthur, *Strange Fire*, 222.

inquire about the following issues when considering "Christian" colleges.

Inspiration of Scripture

Does the college affirm and teach that *all* Scripture is inspired by God? The Bible makes it clear that every word is God-breathed and profitable for teaching, for reproof, for correction, and for training in righteousness (2 Timothy 3:15-17). Any "Christian" college that does not agree (or require its faculty to agree) with this premise is on very shaky spiritual ground. Ask whether the school teaches and accepts the entire Bible, or focuses on selective portions or passages and only in specific Bible classes. The answer may reveal whether the school takes seriously the Christian obligation to teach the whole counsel of God in all areas.

Inerrancy of Scripture

Does the college affirm and teach that the Bible is inerrant in its original writings? This means that God made no mistakes, nor permitted them to be made when Scripture was originally written (Psalm 19:7; 2 Peter 1:20-21). Only through the inerrant Word of God will any student have confidence that he can turn to Scripture for all matters. Find out the school's position concerning the biblical presentation of creation. This area of interpretation may reveal what interpretive approach the student will learn in the classroom.

Infallibility of Scripture

Does the college affirm and teach that God's written Word is infallible, meaning, that it will not fail to accomplish His purpose? (Isaiah 55:11).[188] A college that refuses to accept this truth will not be able to provide hope and confidence in God's plan, which is key for every student who faces questions about life, death, sin, and problems. Inquire how students are encouraged to use the Bible in daily life. A school that pushes students to rely on the Bible in everyday interactions

---

188 *See generally* H.D.M. Spence-Jones, ed. *2 Timothy*, *The Pulpit Commentary* (London: Funk & Wagnalls Company, 1909), 56-57; John Piper, "Thoughts on the Sufficiency of Scripture: What it does and doesn't mean," *Desiring God Ministries*, accessed July 19, 2013, http://www.desiringgod.org/resource-library/taste-see-articles/thoughts-on-the-sufficiency-of-scripture.

likely is one that expects God to do great things through the use and application of His Word.

Authority of Scripture

Does the college teach and affirm that the Bible is authoritative? Every Christian college should agree that since Scripture contains the words of God, and since the words of God are authoritative, Scripture is authoritative.[189] Specifically, the question is whether Scripture is *one* authority (of many), or whether it is *the* authority, which is what the Bible teaches. If it is *the* authority, then it is sufficient to address *all* of life's problems.[190] To disregard it in favor of worldly teaching is folly (Proverbs 14:12; 16:25; 21:2). Does this school view the Bible as similar to other religious texts or writings? The answer will reveal not only whether the school is more interested in truth than in political correctness, but it also will demonstrate whether Scripture will be highly esteemed by the faculty and administration.

Sufficiency of Scripture

Does the college teach and affirm that the Bible is sufficient for all matters of life and godliness? (2 Peter 1:3). Perhaps this issue best sums up whether any particular college (or person) believes in all of the above points. If the Bible is inspired, inerrant, infallible, and authoritative, then it *must* also mean that it contains everything necessary for salvation, life, and godliness.[191] Although many colleges (and individuals) might agree that the Bible is sufficient for salvific and doctrinal purposes, meaning, it teaches people how to be saved and what to believe,[192] many do not affirm its sufficiency for all

---

189 Richard Mayhue, "The Authority of Scripture," *The Master's Seminary Journal* 15, no. 2 (Fall 2004): 232.

190 *See* Heath Lambert, "The Sufficiency of Scripture," *Biblical Counseling Coalition*, accessed July 23, 2013, http://biblicalcounselingcoalition.org/blogs/2012/06/18/the-sufficiency-of-scripture/ ("we should be passionate about sufficiency because God's Word teaches that our authoritative Bible is also our sufficient Bible").

191 Heath Lambert, "Theological Basis of Biblical Counseling II" (Lecture, The Master's College, Santa Clarita, California, July 23, 2013).

192 James White, *Scripture Alone* (Minneapolis, MN: Bethany House, 2004), 32 ("The Scriptures are the sole sufficient, certain, infallible rule of faith for the church—they alone reveal all that is necessary to be believed for salvation and a godly life"); MacArthur, *Strange Fire*, 219 ("Word of God alone is our supreme rule for life and doctrine.").

of life's problems. Every student and parent should require that a Christian college worthy of their time and money affirm that Scripture contains everything mankind needs to know and serve God, and that necessarily includes serving Him in the midst of troubles and all trying circumstances that one might experience. As one author put it, the sufficiency of Scripture means that "Scripture contained all the words of God that He intended His people to have at each stage of redemptive history, and that it now contains all the words of God we need for salvation, for trusting Him perfectly, and for obeying Him perfectly."[193] "The Bible is an adequate guide for all matters of faith and conduct."[194] It is sufficient.[195] A college that disagrees with these statements will not be in a position to transfer wisdom to its students, nor will it provide the one tool that God designed to transform souls (Psalm 19:7-14).[196] In short, the Bible is sufficient "to change people into the likeness of Christ, to the glory of God."[197] This is the point of the college years—as well as every moment in this lifetime. Ask how courses that teach the humanities and social sciences rely on Scripture to form an understanding of anthropology (study of societies, culture, and their development), hamartiology (study of sin and the problems

---

193 Wayne Grudem, *Systematic Theology* (Grand Rapids, MI: Zondervan, 1994), 127.

194 John MacArthur, "Embracing the Authority and Sufficiency of Scripture," in *Think Biblically*, edited by John MacArthur (Wheaton, IL: Crossway, 2003), 22; *see also* The Westminster Confession of Faith (1647), 3rd ed., Lawrenceville, GA: Committee for Christian Education and Publications, 1990 ("The whole counsel of God, concerning all things necessary for his own glory, man's salvation, faith, and life, is either expressly set down in Scripture, or by good and necessary consequence may be deduced from Scripture: unto which nothing at any time is to be added, whether by new revelations of the Spirit, or traditions of men.").

195 Of course, the most important question of all—how does one obtain eternal life?—is also answered in Scripture. "This is eternal life, that they may know You, the only true God, and Jesus Christ whom You have sent" (John 17:3); *see* John Street, "Why Biblical Counseling and Not Psychology?" in *Think Biblically*, 203-220 (Wheaton, IL: Crossway, 2003). Failure to recognize this fact inevitably leads to guesswork about eternity and individual opinions about how to live (Proverbs 21:2). As one author put it, "Speculation will not help us find God, but will only lead us to some idol we have created in our own image." Michael Horton, "The Gospel and the Sufficiency of Scripture," *Modern Reformation*, accessed July 19, 2013, http://www.modernreformation.org/default.php?page=articledisplay&var1=ArtRead&var2=1191&var3=; *see also* John MacArthur, *Rediscovering Expository Preaching* (Dallas, TX: Word Publishing, 1992).

196 MacArthur, "Embracing the Authority and Sufficiency of Scripture," in *Think Biblically*, 30.

197 Jay Adams, *A Theology of Christian Counseling*, (Grand Rapids, MI: Zondervan, 1986), 105.

facing mankind), and soteriology (study of the doctrine of salvation). The answer may reveal whether the school believes the biblical teaching that sin is the cause of human suffering and there is only one cure—repentance, faith, and surrender to Jesus Christ.

A Christian College Should Teach Students a Basic Scriptural Skill Set

If a Christian college affirms the principles set forth above with regard to Scripture, it will be in a position to teach its students some basic skills that every Christian should have. Basic, however, does not mean easy. Students should anticipate, and welcome, the opportunity to be challenged during college. As Thomas Edison is rumored to have said, "The reason a lot of people do not recognize opportunity is because it usually goes around wearing overalls looking like hard work." Spiritual growth follows the same rule in that it comes from a lifetime of striving toward righteousness by doing battle on a daily basis in the spiritual realm (2 Corinthians 10:3-5). A college intent on equipping believers for a lifetime of battle should teach them how to use Scripture in a practical way. Jesus provides the best example of how to do this.

Basic Skill #1: Using Scripture to Resist and Overcome Temptation

Courses of study, faculty reputation, and school rankings are important college considerations. But more important is the ability to resist and overcome temptation. Jesus quoted and relied upon Scripture in resisting the devil (Matthew 4:1-11; Luke 4:1-13). Three times he referred to Scripture in response to three different temptations, prefacing his resistance with the words, "It is written" (Matthew 4:4, 7, 10). Further, he summed up everything that is required for effective resistance in a mere three lines. First, "Man shall not live by bread alone, but by every word that comes from the mouth of God" (Matthew 4:4); this statement provides clear instruction that God's words provide life, and they should be relied upon by His children, even when (or especially when) temptation arises. Second, "you shall not put the Lord your God to the test" (Matthew 4:7); this is a reminder that God's children should be wise and practical, not subjecting themselves to worldly temptations or risks that lead to sin. Third, "You shall worship the Lord your God and him only shall you serve" (Matthew 4:10); this sums up the entire reason behind mankind's existence and God's children will stave off all temptation by focusing on this targeted mission. Does your choice of college move you toward or away from Jesus' example? Will the college help or hurt your chances of being able to resist and overcome temptation through God's Word? Determining whether and how the college teaches its students to use Scripture will provide the answers to these questions.

Basic Skill #2: Using Scripture to Teach

Campus life and fun activities are interesting factors to consider when looking at colleges. However, they do not provide lasting satisfaction or joy. Lasting joy comes from the indwelling Holy Spirit, who prompts believers to teach others the way to eternal life. Using Scripture to teach is consistent with the life of Jesus. He was not prone to giving opinions, relaying anecdotes, or referring to random authors. Instead, he cited the Word of God when he taught his disciples. For example, he not only used it to explain what might appear to be the irrational hatred that his followers would face (John 15:18-25), but he also used it to explain how he had fulfilled Scripture (Luke 24), thereby rendering him alone worthy of the title "Lord." Scripture shows that he truly is *the* way to eternal life (John 14:6).

In light of this, believers would do well to realize that if Scripture is good enough for Jesus to use when teaching, then it is certainly good enough for his followers. Put another way, true followers of Christ will focus primarily on the Word of God when teaching, and not on the latest popular book or "Christian" trend.[198] God's Word is living and active and sharper than any two-edged sword (Hebrews 4:12). Using a dull substitute that the world offers makes no sense. Does the college you are considering rely primarily on those dull substitutes, or does it provide a basis for you to learn from the source of all knowledge and wisdom—in God's Word?

---

198 J. Barton Payne, "Higher Criticism and Biblical Inerrancy," in *Inerrancy*, edited by Norman Geisler (Grand Rapids, MI: Zondervan Publishing House, 1980), 90 ("Gerhard Maier observes, 'the concept that the Bible must be treated like any other book has plunged theology into an endless chain of perplexities and inner contradictions'").

Basic Skill #3: Using Scripture to Warn and Motivate

Many people associate college life with athletics. After all, who hasn't rooted for his favorite college team in the NCAA basketball tournament or in a bowl game? But what if a college provided students with an opportunity to play on the real winning team? What if that school provided an accurate warning of what to watch out for in life as well as motivation for obeying God? Wouldn't this be more important than a strong college football team with a cool mascot? Of course it would.

Jesus referenced Scripture as a warning to those who violate God's commands; at the same time, he motivated believers with a blessing for those who teach obedience (Matthew 5:19). Importantly, this passage follows Jesus' teaching that every word from God's law will be fulfilled, thereby esteeming Scripture and its lasting value (Matthew 5:18).

Jesus' words in this passage should be taken personally. Every believer should determine which type of person he is—one who is ignoring God's commands and teaching others to do the same (by word or example), or one who is keeping God's commands and teaching others to do likewise. The only way to answer that question accurately is to dive into the Word of God in order to discover God's commands, which is precisely the point. Does the college you are considering provide an opportunity to make that plunge into the Word? Or is the weekend football game more important?

Basic Skill #4: Using Scripture to Justify Righteous Conduct

Geography is a big deal. In fact, finding a school in a convenient or beautiful location is something to consider. But if the goal is to be like Christ—and to be near him—perhaps his use of the Word is a more important factor.

Jesus cited Scripture as support for his own righteous conduct, even when that conduct was perceived by others as harsh or offensive (*see* Matthew 21; Mark 11; Luke 19; John 2). Jesus' use of Scripture in this regard should direct believers to assess all actions they are considering in light of Scripture. Put another way, although the much-maligned bumper sticker— "WWJD?"—has somewhat fallen by the wayside over the past few years, asking the question, "What would Jesus do?" (Or better yet, "What did Jesus command his followers to do?"), it is a good measuring stick to use when deciding how God wants His children to live. In the passages quoted above, it is clear that Jesus would act only in accordance with Scripture. Against that backdrop, will the college you attend aid you in acting in accordance with Scripture?

Basic Skill #5: Using Scripture to Highlight Unrighteous Conduct or Thinking

Prospective students often get caught up in what the world thinks about a school, how large of an endowment a school has, or how nice the campus is. In fact, schools highlight these points in their marketing brochures. Jesus, however, used God's Word to highlight something else—sin. And he did so with a sense of grace and urgency that every student should consider when choosing a college.

To put the sin-problem that college students are facing today into perspective, C.S. Lewis once said:

> The greatest barrier I have met is the almost total absence from the minds of my audience of any sense of sin …. The early Christian preachers could assume in their hearers, whether Jews, Metuentes, or Pagans, a sense of guilt …. Thus the Christian message was in those days unmistakably the *Evangelium*, the Good News. It promised healing to those who knew they were sick. We have to convince our hearers of the unwelcome diagnosis before we can expect them to welcome the news of the remedy. The ancient man approached God (or even the gods) as the accused person approaches his judge. For the modern man, the roles are quite reversed.[199]

---

199 C.S. Lewis, *God in the Dock: Essays on Theology and Ethics*, ed. Walter Hooper (Grand Rapids, MI: Eerdmans Publishing Company, 1970), 267; *see also* Jerry Bridges, *Respectable Sins* (Colorado Springs, CO: NavPress), 17.

The only remedy to this lack of awareness is Scripture. Jesus exposed the errors and sinful self-righteousness of religious and cultural leaders by referring them to and citing God's Word, which often led to a parable or explanation that highlighted their incorrect understanding of themselves and the Word (*see, e.g.,* Luke 10:25-37; Mark 7:14-23; Mark 12:18-27). Since believers are to be on the lookout for wolves in sheep's clothing who would lead God's children astray (Matthew 7:15), the most effective means to counter their false teaching is to rely exclusively on Scripture. Specifically, believers run the very real risk of being deceived by false teaching if they fail to examine the pages of Scripture so that counterfeits are readily exposed. Does your college choice prepare you for this danger? Or is it so focused on campus amenities that its students might fall prey to wolves?

Basic Skill #6: Using Scripture to Provide Confidence That Jesus Is the Messiah

Dorm rooms and cafeteria selection are high on the list for most parents when helping children choose a college. After all, no parent wants his child in a filthy setting or not getting enough to eat. But Jesus did not seem particularly concerned with his personal comfort or sustenance. He was confident in the Father's plan, and believing parents should seek that confidence for their children.

Specifically, Jesus quoted Scripture to explain not only what would happen to him in the future (*see* Matthew 26:24, 31; Mark 14:21, 27), but his explanations (with the use of Scripture) proved that he was (is) the Messiah and that all Scripture is fulfilled in him (Luke 24). In light of this, his followers today should be confident that reliance on Scripture to prove that Jesus is the Savior of mankind is not an ill-advised exercise. To the contrary, 1 John was written to provide assurance of salvation, and that salvation is only through Christ Jesus, about whom the pages of Scripture were written (1 John 1:1-4; 1 John 5; *see also* Luke 24:27). Even if the only benefit from knowing and understanding Scripture were the assurance of salvation and a relationship with the Savior, it would be enough. However, the reality is that God's children not only gain assurance and a relationship, but also forgiveness and an inheritance that never ends, "according to the riches of His grace" (Ephesians 1:7). Does the college you are

119

considering seek to provide assurance that Christ is the Savior of mankind? Or does it promote self-esteem and self-reliance instead?

A Christian College Should Place the Goal of Spiritual Growth at the Heart of All Curriculum

In the book of Proverbs, God contrasts two categories of people: foolish and wise. Although no one wants to be called a fool (and certainly no one wants to *be* a fool), the world (and hell) is filled with billions of them. If college is truly a place of learning, then it should be a place where students are given the tools and encouragement to move from one category (the fool) to the other (the wise). How can a prospective student know if the college he is considering is such a place? In other words, is there any biblical counsel related to this issue and the selection of a college?

In the book of Job, mining operations are described for various precious stones and gems, such as gold, silver, copper, sapphire, crystal, and topaz. Job details the processes (the miners "refine," "smelt," "cut channels," and "dam up streams") and the locations (in "flinty rock," "out of the earth," and in "shafts in a valley"). In contrast—and perhaps to the dismay of the hearer—Job asks, "But where shall wisdom be found?" and just as quickly answers that "it is not found in the land of the living" (Job 28:12-13). Not willing to allow his readers to despair, Job's explanation of wisdom provides great hope and guidance to those who yearn for it.

> God understands the way to it,
>   and he knows its place.
> For he looks to the ends of the earth
>   and sees everything under the heavens.
> When he gave to the wind its weight
>   and apportioned the waters by measure,
> when he made a decree for the rain
>   and a way for the lightning of the thunder,
> then he saw it and declared it;
>   he established it, and searched it out.

And he said to man,
  'Behold, the fear of the Lord, that is wisdom,
  and to turn away from evil is understanding.'
  (Job 28:23-28)

In the simplest terms, wisdom is found in knowing God, fearing Him, and following Him. Those believers who desire wisdom must strive for righteousness (Luke 13:24), long for God's Word (1 Peter 2:1-9), and seek to pass down wisdom to future generations (Titus 2). Otherwise, the risk is to fall prey to those false teachers who may seem right, but whose ways end in destruction (2 Peter 2).

A Christian college, therefore, should be a place where spiritual growth is of paramount importance. After all, spiritual growth is just another way of saying sanctification, which is the process of becoming more and more like Jesus by walking in the Spirit. To that end, a Christian college curriculum should seek to glorify God (John 12:28) and to encourage godliness, which is profitable in the present life and also in the life to come (1 Timothy 4:7-8). How many schools can offer such an eternal benefit to their students? Not many. But for those that do, they must bring students on a journey from one level of the Christian walk to the next, moving from babes in the faith to spiritually mature Christians (Colossians 1:28-29; 1 Corinthians 12:11; 1 John 2:12-14). This growth comes through the nourishment of constant training and practice (Hebrews 5:12-14). As one author put it, spiritual growth "comes from reading, meditating on, and submitting to the Word of Christ, allowing the Scriptures to permeate our hearts and minds."[200] College can be part of that process.

Additional Values to Look for in a Christian College

Of course, the list could go on and on in terms of identifying characteristics to look for in a Christian college. Without much controversy, most believers would agree that in addition to learning vocational skills, it would be good for students to graduate

---

200 MacArthur, *Strange Fire*, 206.

- knowing truth (John 8:32)

- understanding the value of prayer and the unnecessary weight of anxiety (Philippians 4:6-7)

- treasuring the things that God treasures (Matthew 6:19-24)

- having pure and worthy thoughts (Philippians 4:8)

- showing themselves to be good examples of believers (1 Timothy 4:12)

- being trained in the way of the Lord (Proverbs 22:6)

- loving others (Luke 6:27-36)

- doing all things without grumbling or disputing (Philippians 2:14)

- performing good works while at the same time speaking evil of no one (Titus 3:1-8)

- shedding sin (Hebrews 12:1)

- giving thanks in all things (1 Thessalonians 5:18)

- making disciples of Jesus Christ by teaching others to obey his commands (Matthew 28:19-20).

The point is, most believing students who have dedicated themselves to learning God's plan for their lives will quickly conclude that the *best* way for this to happen is to sit at the feet of an institution wholly dedicated to God's Word. While there is no approved college list set forth in the Bible, even a cursory reading of the Word will lead prospective students, their parents, and their pastors/elders to a more thoughtful analysis of the available choices than a school website will offer.

CHAPTER 14

PRACTICAL QUESTIONS
AND CONSIDERATIONS

As mentioned above, there is no "one size fits all" response to the question of college choice. However, Christians "must begin with the assumption that there is no area of life where biblical principles are irrelevant."[201] Therefore, although individual circumstances dictate that there are a seemingly endless number of questions that can arise for students and parents, God's Word provides guidance in answering those questions. For example, what if the student does not want to attend a Christian college? What if the student is not a Christian? What if the Christian school is more expensive than a secular school? What if the Christian school does not offer the course of study that interests the student? What if a spouse disagrees with sending the child to a Christian college? What if a student already is enrolled in a secular school? What if ...? What if ...? The list could go on and on. Although not intended to be a comprehensive discussion of every possible question, the following seeks to provide practical biblical counsel and advice to believers who raise or confront some of those issues.

What if the Student Does Not Want to
Attend a Christian College?

This discussion assumes, of course, that a parent is paying for college or somehow has ultimate decision-making authority over a child's college choice. In that situation, although it is wise to consult with a child regarding his college preferences, the ultimate decision should be based on a careful reading of Scripture and the personal conviction that arises from that study. In fact, a disagreement over college choice

---

201 Douglas Wilson, "Scripture Forbids Us to Educate Our Children in the Public Schools," *Center for Reformed Theology and Apologetics,* accessed September 28, 2015, http://www.reformed.org/webfiles/antithesis/index.html?mainframe=/webfiles/antithesis/v2n1/ant_v2n1_issue1.htm.

is a great opportunity for the parent and child to open God's Word together in an effort to understand His plan for the life of His children. All things (including making decisions) should be done to the glory of God—not to the demands of a child (1 Corinthians 10:31; 1 Samuel 2:29-30). However, before simply making a decision and issuing an ultimatum, a parent should understand that kids from families that discuss religion and spirituality at home and who attend worship services together are greatly influenced to agree with their parents' beliefs and decisions.[202] Although sending a child to college might be the last time a parent can "force" that child into an atmosphere of Christian influence and this, in turn, may be just the stimulus the student needs to develop a thirst for God (Psalm 42:1-2), the wise parent will have lived out the gospel over the course of a lifetime and then will seek to involve his child in the biblical decision-making process. That being said, while a child's preferences should be considered carefully and a respectful conversation should occur regarding the issues raised by both sides, a wise Christian parent will seek to honor God before man.[203]

What if the Student Is Not a Christian?

Biblical counsel is for Christians. In fact, this entire book is written with the assumption that readers know God and want to do His will—even if difficult. That said, it is possible that some readers are in families where not all members are believers. For example, a believing parent might be asking what to do with an unbelieving child who is ready to go to college. The answer to this question depends on the Christian

---

202 McKinley Cobb, "Teen Dreams: Church Influences Career Choice," *Crosswalk. com*, accessed January 30, 2016, http://www.crosswalk.com/family/parenting/teens/teen-age-dreams.html.

203 There is nothing that precludes creative thinking in reaching an agreement with a child who prefers to not attend a Christian college. For example, some Christian parents have tried to prepare their children for the world by requiring attendance at a Christian college for at least two years prior to transferring, some have required students to continue living at home while attending secular schools in order for them to remain under Christian influence, some have delayed college altogether in an effort to stimulate the maturation process, and some have even required their children to attend an alternative school for a short period that focuses almost exclusively on theology and spiritual growth in order that they grow in their faith to the point where secular humanism will not be as influential. *See* Kersley Fitzgerald, "What is the Purpose of College?" *Blogos*, accessed September 15, 2015, http://www.blogos.org/thetakeaway/what-is-the-purpose-of-college.html.

college that is being considered. Some Christian colleges require a statement of faith prior to admission. For those colleges, it would be a sin to lie about an applicant's faith just to get admitted (1 John 2:4). Other Christian colleges do not require that students be saved prior to attending. While the commitment of some of those schools to God's Word and to biblical living may be suspect, the wise parent will look carefully at them to determine if the child will be under the influence of solid biblical teaching. If so, such a school might be the best choice. On the other hand, if a child ends up attending a secular school, the wise parent may impose (as part of the deal to send the child to that school) the requirement that the student get involved with Christian clubs on campus and attend church on Sundays. God clearly promises blessings for those who delight in His Word and who avoid imitating the wicked (Psalm 1:1-3). Although there certainly is power in the prayer of a righteous parent (James 5:16), sending a non-Christian child to a secular school with zero Christian influence may be akin to just giving up, depending on the attitude and motivation behind such a decision.

What if the Parent Refuses to Pay for His Child to Attend a Christian College?

The opposite of the above scenario is the Christian student with a parent who refuses to pay for his child's Christian schooling. There are at least two options for the child, and each assumes that he is spiritually mature, theologically sound, and trained in defending the faith. First, the student can seek alternative methods of payment for the Christian college (*e.g.,* loans, scholarships, grants), so that he is not reliant on his parent's money. In this situation, the student must be sure to continue to honor his mother and father as required by God (Exodus 20:12), although honoring a parent does not necessarily mean giving in to a parent's college choice when the student is financially independent and emancipated (not living in the home under the guidance of the parent).[204] Second, the student can attend a secular

---

204 *See* John MacArthur, "Do Adults Still Need to Obey Their Parents?" *Grace to* You, accessed September 23, 2015, https://www.gty.org/resources/bible-qna/BQ082212/do-adults-still-need-to-obey-their-parents (in discussing Colossians 3:20 and Ephesians 6:1, the word *Tekna* "is a general term for children and is not limited to a specific age group. It refers to any child still living in the home and under parental guidance").

school with the knowledge that he will be attending school with an ungodly and potentially hostile group of people, whose lifestyles and beliefs might be harmful to his faith. In that situation, the student must focus intently on living for God in the secular world, seeking fellowship with other believers, being a member of a local church, and engaging in disciplined prayer and Bible study.

What if a Spouse Disagrees with Sending a Child to a Christian College?

In an ideal situation, a husband and wife will be at peace and in agreement on the selection of a school for their college-aged child. If, however, one spouse desires to send the child to a Christian college and the other spouse disagrees with the decision, then a believing spouse who desires such an education for the student should consider a number of issues. First, is the objecting spouse an unbeliever? If so, special care should be taken to not tar the name of Christ in addressing the issue. All conversations should be seasoned with grace and conducted with wisdom (Colossians 4:5-6), and if the objecting spouse is an unbelieving husband, the Christian wife should follow the principles set forth in 1 Peter 3:1-6. Second, (even if both spouses are believers), is the objecting spouse a husband or a wife? While a husband may certainly acquiesce to the desires of his wife on non-essential issues, the Bible teaches that a wife is to submit to her husband (1 Peter 3:1; Ephesians 5:22-24). In fact, a woman with a "gentle and quiet spirit" is "precious" in the sight of God (1 Peter 3:4). Women are equal in value before God (1 Corinthians 11), but they are not to assume the role that God intended for man (*see, e.g.,* 1 Timothy 2:11-15). In Genesis 2, God makes it clear that the woman was made as a helper for man, a companion to ease his loneliness, perfectly suited to him (Genesis 2:18-25). Further, God honors Sarah, who "obeyed Abraham, calling him lord," and commends women to follow this example of obedience (1 Peter 3:6). Therefore, although a husband may (and likely should) consult his wife on a variety of issues, including college choice, an attempt to paint husbands and wives as absolutely equal partners in the final decision-making process ignores their God-given roles. Even so, while a husband might have the final say in choosing a college for his child, a prudent man will consult with his wife, try to understand her position, and seek to find common ground on this issue for the glory of God (1 Peter 3:7). As the saying goes: "Happy wife, happy life" (*see also* Proverbs 21:9).[205] Even more important is the command issued to the husband to "love" his wife and to seek her sanctification, just as Christ loves the church (Colossians 3:19; Ephesians 5:25-26). Cramming a decision down the throat of a spouse likely is *not* the best way to glorify God's name, regardless of gender.

What if the Christian College is More Expensive than a Secular College?

This question can arise in many different scenarios. The Christian school might have higher tuition, the location of the Christian school might be cost prohibitive due to travel or living expenses, or the Christian school might not offer a financial aid package that is as good as one being offered at a secular institution. No matter the reason, a believer who is facing an expensive Christian education should consider at least three issues:

- God calls believers to be wise with their finances (Malachi 3:10; Romans 13:8; Matthew 6:21).

- God calls believers to be good stewards with the money entrusted to them (1 Corinthians 4:2; 1 Timothy 5:8; Hebrews 13:5; Matthew 25:20-21; Luke 12:42-46).

- God calls believers to engage in personal sacrifice to follow Him (Romans 12:1-2).

At first blush, these three issues may appear contradictory when trying to figure out how and where to spend money. After all, wisdom might call for believers to avoid significant debt, but those same believers might think that their money should go to a Christian institution and that personal sacrifice requires them to pay more for a godly education than spending any money for an ungodly one. Yet again, the guidelines for making this decision rest on the pages of Scripture. Although believers must individually wrestle with these issues, their decisions should be made only after consultation with wise counsel

---

205 In many situations, a wise husband will also accept his wife's suggestions and guidance in areas where she has more expertise or knowledge.

(Proverbs 15:22; 22:15). That counsel might call for a student to spend a year or two at a community college (while continuing to practice the spiritual disciplines to guard against worldly influence) in order to save money and complete certain general education requirements, or it might encourage the student to approach his church or the Christian college with the issue in an effort to determine if there are alternatives to racking up debt (for example, through a work-study program, or through different scholarship or grant sources that were not offered initially). Whatever the outcome, the believer must find contentment knowing that he is called to freedom (Galatians 5:13; 1 Peter 2:16; 1 Corinthians 10:23), and that no one is saved (or lost) simply by selecting one particular college over another. Salvation is of the Lord (Psalm 62:1).

What if the Student Has a Specialized Interest Not Offered at a Christian School?

As discussed above, Scripture seems to indicate that spending four formative years in a secular setting at the feet of anti-Christian instructors is *not* God's plan for the majority of believing students. Even if the secular professors are not overtly hostile to Christianity, a student might still be better served sitting under the influence of those who love God. However, there *might* be situations that call for attendance at non-Christian institutions. Just as not all are called to be full-time pastors (or businessmen) and not all are called to major in biblical studies (or economics), not all are required to attend a Christian college.[206] For example, a very specialized course of study might require certain training that is absent or weak in a Christian college. Likewise, a student pursuing a particular major might benefit from using world-class facilities that sometimes are not available at certain Christian schools. Those are exceptions, however. Students should not make the mistake of thinking that they should attend a Christian school only if they desire to go into full-time ministry. All subjects can and should be taught with God's truth as the backdrop. But unless God is

---

206 Notably, not all Christians are called to attend a four-year college (or any college at all). Some, for example, might seek careers that require less schooling, or that cannot be pursued through a Christian college. Each individual will have to assess his life path in accordance with Scripture and be comforted by God's promise that His purpose will not be thwarted (Job 42:2).

left out of the college decision, there is no inherent sin associated with the mere attendance at a secular institution. However, the scriptural principles outlined above should be considered very carefully before a young person ventures out of his parents' day-to-day guidance and into a secular setting. If such a decision is made, special precautions must be taken to protect his heart from the worldly pollution that inevitably will be offered.[207] To be clear, however, nothing in this section should be construed as condoning a non-Christian education or attendance at a secular institution for the vast majority of believing young people. Indeed, foregoing a Christian education during this important period should be the exception, rather than the rule.[208]

As mentioned, there are students who are called into specialized areas of study that may not be offered at a Christian college.[209] How those students should protect themselves at secular institutions has been addressed already (prayer, Bible study, Scripture memorization, fellowship, church membership and attendance, evangelism), but the issue of specialization raises another issue—that of planning. Specifically, Christian students should be thinking strategically about the rest of their lives *before* choosing a college, especially in terms of how they will spend their time *after* college. For example, modern-day Christians often compartmentalize their Christianity separately from their occupations. Some believe that faith is separate from work and so they fail to integrate the two. What they fail to realize, however, is that "no Christian, in any profession, can be happy when torn in two contrary directions."[210] God put it best when He advised that no one

---

207 These would include the requirement to attend church, to be involved in Christian organizations, and to remain in touch with Christian leaders, especially youth pastors. Fuller Youth Institute, "You Make the Call: What College Freshmen Need to Hear from their Youth Pastors," *Sticky Faith*, accessed September 22, 2015, http://stickyfaith.org/articles/you-make-the-call ("[A] factor commonly evident in students who maintain vibrant faith is consistent, quality youth pastors and small group leaders." "Also consistently, these small group leaders remained in touch and involved in their lives across the college transition.").

208 It should not be assumed that Christian colleges do not offer a wide array of majors or professional opportunities. Many are sophisticated and provide a well-rounded education that prepares students for entry into many walks of life, with the added benefit of preparing them to make that entry as mature believers who will represent Christ with honor.

209 There are at least 1,200 majors that have been identified by the College Board. College Board, 2016 *Book of Majors*, ed. Tom Vanderberg (New York: Guidance Publications, 2015).

210 Pearcey, *Total Truth*, 65.

can serve two masters since his allegiance will be torn; one will win out (Matthew 6:24).

With that in mind, college is an excellent time to start thinking about how faith might interact with vocation. Of course, believers should be considering what God's plan is for their lives, but this involves more than thinking about whether or not God intends that His children glorify Him. They should ask, "How can I best serve the Lord through my life's work?"[211] Specifically, college students should be strategic about *how* they intend to glorify God in real life. While consulting Scripture and other believers, students should be considering their aptitudes, desires, abilities, gifts, and opportunities.[212] They should get excited about their service in God's kingdom. For example, a skilled artist might consider how to bring God's message to the world through art; a skilled mechanic might think about how he can be so excellent in what he does that he develops relationships with repeat customers who might be receptive to the gospel message; a skilled teacher might come up with creative ways to tie God's handiwork to her classroom lessons; a skilled businessman might take calculated risks in order to build finances to support overseas missionaries. In short, vocations are "not something *we do for God—which would put the burden on us to perform and achieve. Instead, it is a way we participate in God's work.* "[213] Knowing that a great many years might be spent in a specific profession, prospective college students must take more than a moment to consider their strengths and talents so that they can then consider the courses of study that will be offered at particular schools and whether the faculty will encourage them to make strategic plans to serve God upon graduation. True Christians will be on the battlefield in every moment, so they need to ensure that they are being reinforced with truth.

---

211 Friesen, *Decision Making and the Will of God*, 340.

212 Ibid., 338.

213 Pearcey, *Total Truth*, 50; *see also* Tozer, *The Pursuit of God*, 120 ("Let every man abide in the calling wherein he is called and his work will be as sacred as the work of the ministry. It is not what a man does that determines whether his work is sacred or secular, it is why he does it. The motive is everything.").

What if the Student Has No Choice or Already Is Enrolled at a Secular School?

When John the Baptist was asked by soldiers what they should do in response to his message of repentance, he counseled them to not extract money by way of violence or lies, and to be content with their wages (Luke 3:14). He did not instruct them to stop being soldiers. When vile tax collectors asked for guidance, he simply told them to not collect more than was authorized by the law (Luke 3:12-13). He did not instruct them to stop collecting taxes. And when the crowds asked how they should respond to the message, he instructed them to share with those in need (Luke 3:10-11). He did not force them into or out of any particular trade or profession. In other words, God expects people to grow where they are planted.

Like the soldiers and tax collectors, there might be students who already are attending secular colleges and are wondering if doing so is sin. Their struggle might further be complicated by the fact that they believe they are called into particular professions or courses of study that are not available through Christian colleges, which is addressed in the previous section.

As with most of these questions, it depends on the student. For example, Daniel, Shadrach, Meshach, and Abednego did not refuse a Babylonian education, but they were steadfast in their commitment to the one, true God, and were wise beyond their years (*see* Daniel 1). They were bold and dedicated, even when facing death (Daniel 1-3). Their compulsory participation in the secular education is not condemned in Scripture, but their lifestyles never conformed to that of the sinful Babylonians. They were mature, believing students who recognized when to seek alternatives from the demands placed on them.

On the other hand, a diligent study of Scripture might lead a modern-day student to believe that a change in schools is the wisest course of action. Such a decision brings a number of other scriptural principles into play. For example, God desires that His children be financially responsible (Proverbs 27:23-24; Luke 14:28; 1 Corinthians 14:40). If dropping out of one school and enrolling in another leaves the student (or his parents) in a financially unstable position or unable to repay debt that already has been incurred, then such a move probably is *not* the right choice (Ecclesiastes 5:5; Romans 13:7-8; Psalm 37:21). Similarly, God may have gifted a student with a unique business acumen that will place him in a position where he can support his local church and a number of missionaries or other Christian organizations at an extraordinary level. If such a student, for example, is at the tail end of his business degree at a respected college, and dropping out will significantly reduce his ability to give, then unless his conscience—as molded by Scripture—leads him to make a change, the wisest choice may be to complete his current studies.[214]

Of course, each of these scenarios contemplates a mature believer who can withstand (and who has proven an ability to withstand) worldly temptations and teachings. A student should not assume that he can handle such temptations on his own. If temptation to sin is too much for a student to handle, he should flee it (Genesis 4:7; 1 Corinthians 10:14; 6:18; 1 Timothy 6:11; 1 Timothy 2:22). Specifically, even when remaining in a school seems the correct thing to do from a personal standpoint, if doing so will bring dishonor to God by way of the student's conduct or attitude, then foregoing personal opportunities might be the way the student dies to self and lives for Christ (Mark 8:35). Put another way, although God will not allow a believer to be tempted beyond his ability to withstand it and God will provide a way of escape (1 Corinthians 10:13), the "way of escape" might involve leaving a secular college campus.

If a Christian student does decide to continue in his studies at a secular college, he should analyze his life to ensure that he is being purposeful about his walk with God and, importantly, about evangelism. Indeed,

---

214 The potential for personal financial gain cannot be the primary reason for attending a non-Christian college, and anyone using a potentially high salary as a reason for secular studies would do well to remember the warning that Jesus gave to the rich (Matthew 19:24, "It is easier for a camel to go through the eye of a needle than for a rich person to enter the kingdom of God"). Although there undoubtedly are individuals who are blessed with the spiritual gift of generosity and have an unwavering focus on generosity and earning for the kingdom (Romans 12:8), the far more common experience is for people to hoard for themselves on earth and only give out of their excess and when it costs them nothing (2 Timothy 3:2). Believers need to be reminded of Christ's command to "lay up for yourselves treasures in heaven" (Matthew 6:20).

evangelism was the Apostle Paul's goal in life when interacting with non-believers (1 Corinthians 9:19). A Christian student also should pray earnestly for the school's faculty and students. College is a mission field. As the Lord spoke through the prophet Jeremiah to the Jews who had been taken to Babylon, "But seek the welfare of the city where I have sent you into exile, and pray to the LORD on its behalf, for in its welfare you will find your welfare" (Jeremiah 29:7). Christian students should seek to shine light in secular schools and should seek God's favor on behalf of those who attend.[215]

In addition, a student who decides to stay enrolled in a secular college must guard against corrupting influences. Daniel, Shadrach, Meshach, and Abednego purposed to not defile themselves with the Babylonian king's food and wine, knowing that such a stand could lead to their deaths (Daniel 1). Daniel refused to stop praying to God and was cast into a den of hungry lions (Daniel 6). Likewise, Daniel's three friends refused to bow down to an idol, and were cast alive into a fiery furnace for their stance (Daniel 3). Although God saved them, the point is that they were willing to suffer in this lifetime for their faith, even to the point of death. A Christian student at a secular college might not be tossed into an oven, but he might have to pass on social opportunities, he might be graded unfairly by professors, and he might become the laughingstock of the classroom or campus. In those situations, believers should count all of their suffering as joy and simply remain steadfast in the faith (James 1:2-4).

Finally, a Christian student at a secular college must be discerning about information being conveyed to him by professors. Christians are to be on guard against deceptive philosophy and are not to be

---

215 For those believers who think they can pass through the crucible of secular college unscathed, they must remember Jesus' warning that true followers will be hated by the world just as they first hated him (John 15:18; Matthew 10:22). Accordingly, Christians attending a secular college must prepare themselves to stand firm and spread the truth in love—and suffer for it—or they will be relegated to just another lukewarm soul joining the multitude who do more harm to the work of the Body than those vehemently against it. After all, "no snowflake in an avalanche ever feels responsible," even though it is participating in mass destruction. The point is, if an individual is not part of the solution, he is part of the problem. In this case, the solution is to spread the gospel of Jesus Christ, and the problem is standing against that message either by act or omission. No matter where one chooses to attend college, he must take a stand for Christ. There is no middle ground (Revelation 3:16).

conformed to the world (Romans 12:2; 2 Corinthians 10:3-5).[216] A Christian student at a secular institution must search God's Word to be sure what he is learning is consistent with God's message (Acts 17:11). In addition to being discerning, a Christian student at a secular institution should be cognizant of the fact that at least two-thirds of Christian students leave the church when they become adults, and this often relates to the teaching (or lack of teaching) they receive while in college. With that dark prospect serving as motivation, a believer in a secular college should be sure to supplement his studies with prayer, time in God's Word, and fellowship.[217]

What if the Student Is a Mathematics, Engineering, or Science Major?

Some argue that the mathematics, engineering, and science departments cover disciplines that are taught objectively and, therefore, are not subject to the same secular biases and ungodly worldviews that infect departments charged with teaching humanities courses such as literature, philosophy, religion, and anthropology. They contend that a secular education in these areas is not fraught with the same perils as liberal arts majors. While courses at secular institutions that involve mathematics may appear spiritually neutral, the reality is that all college students are required to take courses in a variety of subject areas to fulfill their general education requirements. Such courses will expose students to worldly thinking and influences such as those discussed above.[218] Additionally, survey results demonstrate that the degree to which students are committed to their religious beliefs varies by field of study, with humanities students finding religion to be

---

216 Jason Lisle, "Surviving Secular College," *Answers in Genesis*, accessed September 23, 2015, https://answersingenesis.org/college/surviving-secular-college/.

217 Ibid.

218 Likewise, it is very difficult for a Christian who is a science student to find a college that includes a biblical six-day creation account in its statement of faith. According to one tally, there are a few such choices for a biology major, there are one or two for a physics or geology major, and there are none for an astronomy major. *See* Ibid. (Dr. Lisle is an Ohio Wesleyan University *summa cum laude* graduate who double-majored in physics and astronomy, and who minored in mathematics. He later did graduate work at the University of Colorado where he earned a Master's degree and a Ph.D. in astrophysics. He has authored a number of works in both secular and creation literature, including books on astronomy and creationism. He believes in the literal six day creation account described in Genesis); *see also* Steve Golden, "Creation on Campus," *Answers*, October-December 2014, 74-79.

personally helpful in much greater numbers than science students.[219] Put another way, while studying the sciences may insulate students from certain religious discussions, it appears to do so by numbing them to the relevance of spirituality in their lives. Finally, even if a student could avoid affirmative attacks on Christianity, having a Christian worldview means that *everything* should bend to the Word, including mathematics and science. Nothing is spiritually neutral and the absence of God means, by definition, that something is godless. In other words, how can one study without light (or without the Light)? Such an education will lack complete truth to some degree. In short, there is no escape from Satan's tainting influence on a secular campus, even in the more "objective" areas of study. As such, the decision to select one of these college majors, by itself, is insufficient reason to bypass a Christian education.[220]

Does Gender Have Any Role in Choosing a College?

In terms of choosing a college, a man seeking to glorify and know God should go through the same analysis as a woman seeking to glorify and know God. Some might argue, however, that a Christian woman's role is to care for and raise a family, while a Christian man's role is to support his family financially.[221] According to this reasoning, the woman is more apt to benefit from a Christian college that might have courses designed to prepare her for the female role in a family than a man whose goal is to become marketable in a job search. This sort of thinking misunderstands roles and education.

---

219 Astin and Astin. "Spirituality in Higher Education."

220 As John MacArthur put it, "A person who has a secular education doesn't really have a full education because unless you have a biblical worldview that starts with creation by God, you don't understand the way the world is, you don't understand the way reality is, you don't get it and unless you have a biblical view of what is right and what is wrong, you don't know what right is or what wrong is." "The only truly educated person is the person who is educated in the Word of God, and every other discipline is connected to the Scriptures." "Those are the kinds of people who can impact the world for the Kingdom of God." John MacArthur, "MacArthur on Education—Proper Education," The Master's College, accessed July 28, 2015, https://www.youtube.com/watch?v=Qjx-hVbcgDA.

221 This, of course, assumes that all women and all men will get married, which is not necessarily the case.

First, it is true that the Bible instructs married women with children to be diligent at home (Titus 2:3-4). In fact, God praises the woman who cares for her family by keeping her house and affairs in order (Proverbs 31). Although a career outside the home is not her primary concern, this same woman may engage in business activities for the benefit of her family (Proverbs 31:16, 18, 24, 25). A solid Christian college will have majors and classes designed to help its female students become such godly women. Even if a woman remains unmarried, a Christian education designed to help her become more like Christ is preferable to one that simply fills her head with secular knowledge without regard to God.

Second, those who think that a Christian man's sole job is to provide financially for his family are wrong. Although he is to provide for his family (1 Timothy 5:8), he also is to love and cherish his wife (Ephesians 5:25-28; Colossians 3:19), he is to be patient and forgiving (1 Corinthians 13:4; Ephesians 4:32), and he is to wisely govern his household and raise the children (1 Timothy 3:3-5; Ephesians 6:4). A solid Christian college will recognize the great responsibility placed on a man and will, in addition to preparing him for the job market, train him to live a godly life in his own family. A secular school will not.

What if the Student Is Offered an Academic Scholarship at a Secular College?

Praise God for academic prowess. But for the fall of mankind and the resultant taint on our intellect, we all would have more understanding due to a closer relationship with the God of all knowledge (*see, e.g.,* Romans 1:21-22). Even with the fall, however, there are a number of people who have been blessed with higher than average intellectual abilities and/or who work significantly harder than others to separate themselves from the academic pack. Some of these individuals receive scholarship offers from secular institutions based on their academic achievement and standardized test scores. Biblical counsel for these individuals and their parents is similar to the counsel provided to all believers considering college. They should not be caught up solely by the reward of personal achievement (Philippians 2:3). They should consider the impact of their college choice on their finances (Malachi

3:10; Romans 13:8; Matthew 6:21). They should seek wise counsel before making decisions (Proverbs 15:22; 22:15). If a solid Christian school offers the same course of study, a believer might inquire of that school as to whether it will match the support being offered by the secular institution. The point is that a Christian should not make a final decision without considering all facts and available options (Proverbs 19:2). And he should find freedom in his decision if reached with God's glory in mind (1 Corinthians 10:31).

What if the Student Is Offered a Sports Scholarship at a Secular College?

First, there is nothing that requires a student to play sports. Athletic involvement is a voluntary decision and it should never be used as an excuse to not seek God's glory in every situation (1 Corinthians 10:31). Second, while there is nothing inherently sinful about sports, many Christians (when asked to list the benefits of sports) talk about the physical aspects of the game, yet they have no in-depth understanding of how sports might relate to spiritual life. Even if they make the connection between sports and glorifying God, the connection rarely relates to godliness or worship; rather, it mainly is associated with athletic production and achievement.[222] Christian athletes often are confused since they are required to talk tough, hit hard, then point a finger to heaven or bend a knee after a score.[223] Many traits touted in sports (a desire to crush opponents, a mandate to be self-centered, etc.) are often unbiblical. Third, while references to athletic competition fill the pages of Scripture (*see, e.g.,* Genesis 30:8; 32:24; 2 Samuel 2:14; 1 Corinthians 9:24-27; Philippians 3:13-14; Galatians 2:2; Ephesians 6:12; Hebrews 12:1-4) and athletics are even used as a metaphor for the Christian life (2 Timothy 2:5), it is clear that the pursuit of godliness is far more important than winning on the athletic field (1 Corinthians 9:25; 1 Timothy 4:7-8).[224] Finally, Christians can come to

---

222 Shirl James Hoffman, "Sports Fanatics: How Christians have succumbed to the sports culture—and what might be done about it," *Christianity Today*, accessed June 20, 2015, http://www.christianitytoday.com/ct/2010/february/sports-fanatics-football-shirl-hoffman.html.

223 Ibid.

224 David Prince, "Are youth sports a friend or foe of Christian discipleship?" *The Ethics and Religious Liberties Convention of the Southern Baptist Convention*, accessed June 20, 2015, https://erlc.com/article/are-youth-sports-a-friend-or-foe-of-christian-discipleship.

different opinions on the issue of athletics. For example, Eric Liddell, the Olympic runner who loved competition but who refused to run in the 1924 Olympics on the Sabbath, stated in the film, *Chariots of Fire,* "I believe that God made me for a purpose. But he also made me fast, and when I run, I feel his pleasure."[225] For him, athletic pursuit was a way to glorify God, not neglect Him. On the other hand, his sister considered sports to be a waste of time. There are many who consider work advancing the gospel to be a much better way to glorify God than participating in sports.[226]

With the above in mind, it is clear that the decision must be made by each individual in consultation with Scripture. Indeed, a Christian student who is offered a sports scholarship at a secular college must start the analysis the same way that he should start any analysis, by asking, "What decision would bring God the most glory?" Also, if that same student has an opportunity to play at a Christian college, he should inquire of the coaching staff to determine how it integrates faith with athletics. Some teams at Christian colleges are viewed as separate enterprises whose coaches have a watered-down faith or a strange theological understanding of sports (perhaps thinking that victory on the field is akin to being more blessed or becoming more godly through triumph and power). Assuming those questions are answered biblically, a student who has different options may find that a Christian college is the better choice, even for an athlete. Spiritual growth is far more important than muscle development or athletic achievement (1 Timothy 4:7-8).

---

225 Colin Welland, *Chariots of Fire*, Warner Bros. Pictures, 1981. DVD. Warner Home Video, 1992.
226 Prince, "Are youth sports a friend or foe of Christian discipleship?"

CHAPTER 15

A SUMMARY OF BIBLICAL GUIDANCE

To this point, I have attempted to walk students and parents through scriptural principles to consider when making the college choice. After explaining what comprises the overall college experience, the discussion began with the factors typically considered when selecting a school; it conveyed differing worldviews and why those differences matter; it explained how the Bible defines success and education; it warned against evil influence and activity; it specified proper pursuits and the role of parents in the decision; it discussed the issue of stewardship; it warned against dangers such as unstable teaching, filthy education, and overtly hostile professors; it dealt with various objections and practical considerations; it explained what to look for in a Christian college; and it acknowledged that there is not a "one-size-fits-all" answer to the issue of college choice. Overarching this entire discussion is one objective truth—that the perfect, infinite, loving, wise, merciful, gracious, creator God demands and deserves that *all* decisions be made with His glory in mind. To say that there is much for believers to consider from the previous discussion would be an understatement.

In an effort to synthesize the above discussion into a manageable list, the following is a brief summary of a number of principles that Christians should consider when trying to select a college. This list does not address many practical issues, such as geography or finances. Those are addressed elsewhere. Nor is this list designed to help students choose solely among *Christian* colleges; that discussion is contained in the next chapter. It is simply a list of spiritual concepts people should think about when beginning the process, whether they are considering Christian or secular schools, or both. Although some of the questions set forth below may seem unanswerable, and the believer's responsibility is not to predict the future with 100% accuracy, this list is provided to help you start the process and to make the best decision you can with the information you have available to you.

- God's Glory. Which decision brings the most glory to God? If you are unsure, does an objective analysis lead you to believe that one choice likely is the better one when considering how your life will glorify God during the next four years? Are you confident that the values important to your decision reflect biblical values and priorities? Have you sought counsel from your pastor or elders to confirm that your evaluation is consistent with Scripture? (1 Corinthians 10:31; Colossians 3:17)

- Sanctification. Will the school you choose aid you in the process of sanctification, or will the environment hinder your walk with God? Will a college experience that involves attending this school help you know, understand, and obey God better? Which school experience will most likely lead to more righteous living? (1 Thessalonians 4:3-5; 5:23; 2 Timothy 2:21; Leviticus 20:8; Jeremiah 9:23-24; Psalm 119:30)

- Guidance. What counsel do your parents, your church leaders, and other Christians give about choosing a college? Is that counsel based on Scripture? Are you willing to listen to that counsel? (Proverbs 12:15; 15:22)

- Stewardship. Which choice most demonstrates that you are being a good steward of the resources that God has entrusted to you, including your mind, your money, your time, and (if you are a parent) your child? Which college experience will most likely foster maximum spiritual growth over the next four years? (Colossians 3:23; Matthew 25:14-30; Proverbs 16:3)

- Talents/Vocation. Which school curriculum and environment will best develop your talents in such a way as to maximize your ability to serve the Body of Christ? Will those talents be developed at the expense of your morality or biblical way of thinking? Is there a school choice that will allow you to hone your skills while at the same time guard you from worldly corruption? (Romans 12:6-8; Matthew 25:14-30; Exodus 35:10; Jeremiah 17:10)

- <u>Influence.</u> Which school will expose you to the most truth? Which school will likely provide you with the most godly student influence? If your choice will consistently subject you to unrighteousness, whether from faculty or fellow students, how mature are you in the Christian faith? Are you well-prepared in Christian apologetics? Are you morally strong and able to withstand temptation? Will you be influenced, or will you be the influencer? Are you committed to engage in the spiritual disciplines to ensure that your faith is bolstered by God's Word, the Holy Spirit, and other believers while you are in college? (1 Peter 3:15-16; Jude 1:3; Hebrews 5:14)

- <u>Practical Life Skills.</u> Will your school experience foster biblical discernment? Will your studies encourage the pursuit of wisdom? (Hebrews 5:14; James 1:5)

- <u>Scripture.</u> Will attending this school hinder or discourage you from studying God's Word? Will it encourage such study, either expressly or by providing you with sufficient free time to read the Bible? Which school experience will lead you to esteem God's Word as inspired, inerrant, infallible, authoritative, and sufficient? Which school experience will best enable you to become equipped to accurately handle God's Word? (2 Timothy 2:15; 3:15-17; Psalm 19:7-14)

- <u>Thinking.</u> Will attending this school help align your thinking more closely with God's thinking? Will the school experience encourage you to think unbiblically? (Philippians 4:8; Romans 8:5-6)

- <u>Focus.</u> Does the school you are considering encourage self-centeredness or service of others? Will you be tempted to seek personal gain or achievement to the exclusion or detriment of others? (Philippians 2:3-5)

- <u>Evangelism.</u> Will attending this school lead you to evangelize more or less? Will attending this school impact your ability, desire, and commitment to carry out the Great Commission? (Matthew 28:19-20; Mark 16:15)

141

- <u>Pursuits.</u> What does your choice of school indicate that you are pursuing? Are your pursuits leading you toward or away from God? (Matthew 6:33; James 1:11)

- <u>Stability.</u> Does this school promote stable teaching, grounded in truth? If your choice of schools does not, how will you be impacted by unstable or false teaching in the classroom? (James 1:8; Deuteronomy 6:4-9)

- <u>Morality.</u> Does this school promote purity, or does it celebrate filth? How able are you to withstand worldly temptation, and are you prepared to do so? (Matthew 5:8; Colossians 3:5; 12-14; Revelation 22:11-12)

Perhaps the most piercing question any believer can ask (or be asked) when considering a college is this: "Why do you want to attend this school?" The answer will show a deep regard and consideration of God's Word, or it will not. It will focus on spiritual concerns, or it will not. It will demonstrate a careful analysis of the heart issues associated with such a big decision, or it will not. In short, answering the "Why?" question will reveal whether or not a student is choosing a college for the glory of God. And since God's glory must be primary goal for every believer in every decision, the answer to that question is of utmost importance in the college selection process.

CHAPTER 16

THE CHRISTIAN COLLEGE CHECKLIST

This checklist is designed specifically for parents and students trying to choose a *Christian* college, not a secular school. No person can identify the precise Christian college for every student to attend. There is no chapter in the Bible linking specific college names with specific believers. The truth is, there is not *one* correct choice. This is one of the wonderful freedoms believers have been given with their faith (Galatians 5:13). As discussed above, however, there are biblical principles that can be employed to determine God's will on issues not specifically discussed in the Bible, including college choice.[227]

In light of this, a Christian student and his parents should consider the following checklist when trying to choose a Christian college.[228] Of course, certain categories in this list may run counter to those the world offers, since secular lists focus almost exclusively on personal happiness, as opposed to personal holiness.[229]

---

227 *See* Ed Welch, "When Scripture Seems Silent," *CCEF*, accessed March 30, 2015, http://www.ccef.org/resources/blog/when-scripture-seems-silent.

228 This discussion contemplates that a Christian student will avoid a compromised Christian college since, although it does not outright reject the Bible, its views may be seductive and confusing (2 Corinthians 11:3; Matthew 15:7-9; Revelation 3:16).

229 If the decision has been made to attend a secular college, then it is assumed that there is a specific and God-centered reason for doing so, and there is a specific college already chosen. If the reason for making the secular choice is not God-centered, then the decision should be reassessed. If a specific college has not yet been chosen, then one should ask whether he is choosing the secular route for the right reasons, or whether he has simply rationalized his choice and left his options open. After all, if the supposed reason for choosing a secular college is due to a specific course of study not otherwise offered at a Christian college, then it should be safe to assume that the options are quite limited. Otherwise, the odds are that the course of study can also be found in a Christian setting. The only further inquiry at the secular campus level should focus on the existence of Christian organizations on campus, the availability of Christian fellowship and support, the level of hostility the Christian will face for his beliefs, and what steps can be taken to ensure that the student is not ensnared by the sin that so easily entangles and which will be so freely available in the secular college setting (Hebrews 12:1).

Spiritual Essentials

Although not intended to be a comprehensive discussion of each point, this category includes a number of spiritual essentials that should be considered when selecting a Christian college.

- God-centered. Does this college encourage its students to know and seek God? (Jeremiah 29:13; Matthew 6:33). Does this college encourage its students to praise God? (Psalm 35:18; 1 Peter 2:9). Does this college acknowledge God as the Creator of the universe? (Genesis 1:1; Psalm 104; Nehemiah 9:6; Romans 11:36; Revelation 4:11)

- Sovereignty of God. Does this college affirm the sovereignty of God? (Psalm 115:3; Proverbs 16:9)

- Truth and Wisdom. Does this college teach truth? (John 8:32; Hebrews 13:9; Titus 2:1). Does this college teach students the value of godly wisdom? (Proverbs 3:13-18; 24:3-7; Luke 21:15)

- Scripture. Does this college teach that all Scripture is inspired by God and profitable? (2 Timothy 3:15-17). Does this college teach that the Bible is inerrant in its original autographs? (Psalm 19:7; 2 Peter 1:20-21). Does this college teach that Scripture is infallible, meaning, it will not fail to accomplish God's purpose? (Isaiah 55:11). Does this college teach that the Bible, as God's Word, is authoritative? (2 Timothy 3:16-17; Matthew 5:17-18; Proverbs 14:12; 16:25; 21:2). Does this college teach that the Bible is sufficient for all matters of life and godliness? (2 Peter 1:3; Psalm 19:7-14)

- Love. Does this college encourage its students to love one another? (Luke 6:27-36)

- Equipping the Body. Does this college encourage diligent training in the Scriptures in order to build up the Body of Christ? (2 Timothy 2:15; Ephesians 4:11-12)

- Spiritual growth. Does this college emphasize the spiritual growth of its students? (Colossians 1:28-29; 1 Corinthians 12:11; 1 John 2:12-14)

- Righteousness and Holiness. Does this college encourage students to pursue righteousness by living a life in obedience to God? (John 14:21). Does this college teach students how to resist temptation? (James 4:7). Does this college teach students how to live a holy life? (1 Peter 1:15-16; Philippians 4:8; 1 Timothy 4:12)

- Discipleship. Does this college encourage students to make disciples, teaching them to obey God's commands? (Matthew 28:19-20)

- Fellowship. Does this college provide regular opportunities for fellowship with other believers? Does this college provide mature believers who can disciple students? Does this college direct students to commit to a local church and emphasize the spiritual authority of the pastors/elders in the local church? (Hebrews 10:25; Proverbs 27:17)

- Prayer and Trust. Does this college encourage students to pray and to trust God? (Philippians 4:6-7; Proverbs 3:5-6; Psalm 56:3-4)

- Treasure. Does this college encourage students to store up treasures in heaven? (Matthew 6:19-24)

- Attitude and Speech. Does this college teach students to not grumble or complain and, instead, to have pure and noble and thankful thoughts? (Philippians 2:14; 4:8; 1 Thessalonians 5:18). Does this college encourage righteous speech by its students? (Titus 3:1-8)

- Statement of Faith and Faculty. Does this college have a statement of faith that affirms core Christian doctrines, such as the Trinity, the sinful nature of man, the saving work of Christ, the role and identity of the Church, and the return of Christ? Does this college require its faculty to ascribe to its doctrinal and faith statements?[230]

---

230 Of course, the list could go on and on in terms of specifics, and students should be encouraged to delve into individual questions with Christian schools they are considering. These might include inquiries on the schools' views on the creation account, homosexuality, abortion, the presence of non-Christian students on campus, etc.

Non-Spiritual Essentials

Although all issues can be considered "spiritual" and can implicate spiritual matters, the following checklist contains items not specifically addressed in the Bible but which should be considered when choosing among Christian colleges.

- Cost and Financial Aid. Does this college offer an affordable tuition, or will attending put the student in so much debt that it would be irresponsible to enroll? Does this college offer affordable housing? When considering debt, how long will it take to pay off and will it be a huge burden to a student's family? Has the college implemented tuition hikes in the recent past that allow a student to accurately gauge how much his education will cost?

- Course of Study. Does this college offer majors that the student would like to pursue and is the program academically sufficient? If a student changes his mind during college, does this college offer a sufficient number of alternative majors?

- Entrance Requirements. What is the application deadline for this college? What grades, tests, and test scores are required? Does the student qualify? If not, what is the student willing to do to work toward those entrance requirements?

- Accreditation. Is this college accredited and, if so, by which accrediting bodies? What denomination does the school align itself with?

Non-Essentials (But Perhaps Still Important)

These issues might not be "essential" when selecting a Christian college, but one or more of these might still be very important to the decision.

- Location. Is this college located in or near a city where the student would like to live? How close is this college to home if the student wants to make weekend trips? If the student gets a job in or near that city, will he be comfortable living there long-term? Does the student like the weather in this area?

- Environment. Does the student like the campus? Is it large or small? Is it clean? Is it safe? Is it co-ed? How many students attend? Is it more of a commuter college, or do students typically socialize and live on or near campus? Do students stay indoors or outdoors mostly? Is it rural or urban? Does the student have a preference on these points?

- Relationships. Does the student know anyone already attending the school or who will go with the student? Does the student know anyone who lives near the school?

- Student Body. Does this college seem to have a student body consisting of well-rounded believers who are serious about their faith and who find joy in the Lord?[231]

- Diversity. Is the student body and/or faculty ethnically or otherwise diverse?

- Recommendations. Has the student spoken to others who have attended this college? What do they say about it? Do they recommend it? Does the student respect their input?

- Academics. How large are the classes? What is the typical class size and what is the student-to-faculty ratio? Are the professors well-known in their fields? What level of education have they achieved? What have they published? How high does the school rank?

- Professors. Are they approachable? Are they accessible to students? Do the current students seem to like them and their methods of teaching?

---

231 Not only will students likely forge deep friendships during college, but spouses often meet during that time period. *See* Cara Newlon, "College Students Still Often Find Spouses on Campus," USA Today, accessed September 30, 2015, http://www.usatoday.com/story/news/nation/2013/10/15/college-marriage-facebook/2989039/; Scott Croft, "Biblical Dating: How It's Different from Modern Dating," *Boundless*, accessed September 30, 2015, http://www.boundless.org/relationships/2012/biblical-dating-how-its-different-from-modern-dating.

- Graduation Rates. What are the odds that the student will graduate from this college? How long will it take?[232]

- Internships and Jobs. Is the school located near a city or other location where the student can participate in an internship in his course of study? What is the job placement rate after graduation?

- Electives. Does the school offer electives that the student finds interesting and/or challenging?

- Education Abroad. Does the school offer an education abroad program or does it affiliate with another program to allow students that opportunity?

- Rules. Does the school enforce rules on and/or off campus that will cause the student to rebel, whether by deed or attitude?

- Dormitory and Cafeteria. Is the dorm experience what the student is looking for? What types of food options are available on campus? Is there a cafeteria and is the food good?

- Medical Care. Are there on-campus medical services? Does the student have a particular physical or emotional condition that needs to be considered when deciding to attend this college?

- Clubs. Does the school have any extra-curricular clubs that the student would like to join?

- Extra-curricular. Does the college have an athletics department? Does the college have a speech and drama department? Will the student participate?

- Visit. Has the student visited the campus and does he want to attend?

---

232 Overall, less than 60% of college students graduate within six years. Blaire Briody, "11 Public Universities with the Worst Graduation Rates," *The Fiscal Times,* accessed November 10, 2014, http://www.thefiscaltimes.com/Articles/2012/05/17/11-Public-Universities-with-the-Worst-Graduation-Rates.

CHAPTER 17

WHAT IF I'M STILL NOT SURE

Three categories of people might still be struggling with the college decision. The first group might just not like the biblical counsel set forth above. The second group is trying to decide between a Christian and non-Christian education. The third group is simply trying to decide between two or more Christian colleges.

For the reader who might find the counsel in this book difficult to adopt, and if he finds himself conforming to the world's pattern and values when selecting a college, he should ask the following question: "Am I being transformed by renewing my mind through the diligent study and application of Scripture?" If not, read Paul's instruction to those who will one day be face to face with the almighty God: "Do not be conformed to this world, but be transformed by the renewal of your mind, that by testing you may discern what is the will of God, what is good and acceptable and perfect" (Romans 12:2). God is good (Psalm 100:5). Trust Him and His counsel (Psalm 19:7-14).

As to the second category, someone might tell a parent that he should not be arming the enemy with his own child's mind and life and, thus, a Christian education is the only way to go. Another will argue that passing the test of a secular education is the best way for a believing young person to grow. One Christian leader stated the arguments that he heard on either side in this way: "The argument for the [Christian college] people was, 'You can't go into a cold spiritual icebox like [the secular college] and come out spiritually hot,' and the argument on the other side was, 'You can't go into a hothouse like [the Christian college] and come out and face the cold wintry blast of the world.'"[233]

While there is freedom in Christ (Galatians 5:13), that freedom is to no longer be enslaved by sin. Further, although all things are permissible,

---

233 Collin Hansen, "The Holy and the Ivy," *Christianity Today*, accessed April 13, 2015, http://www.christianitytoday.com/ct/2005/september/26.64.html?start=5.

not all things are helpful in a believer's life (1 Corinthians 6:12). Believers are called to not err on the side of potential sin. In other words, the safest course of action always is to choose the path that clearly is not offensive to God (Romans 14:23). If a college cannot be selected with a clear conscience, then it should not be selected. Likewise, if a parent or student is unsure, why not pick a Christian college simply to be a good steward and, at a minimum, to give money to an institution that is committed to God's work? Or why not adopt a hybrid approach—selecting a Christian college that provides a one or two year foundational program with the option of transferring those college credits to another school—before making a final commitment to four years at a particular institution?

As to the final group trying to choose among Christian schools, just choose already! So long as your choice is regulated by scriptural principles, there is freedom in the ultimate decision. (This assumes, of course, that a careful analysis has been done as described above.) Nothing will thwart God's purpose (Job 42:2; Romans 8:28), and believers are saved by grace, through faith, not by choosing a particular college (Ephesians 2:8-10). God simply desires that His children be faithful.[234]

To illustrate this point, there is a story of a man who was asked by God to push a giant rock, which he did day after day, but it never moved. He began to wonder why God had given him an impossible task. One day, God stopped by to check on the man, and the man cried out, "Lord, I have failed. I have not moved the rock." The Lord responded with a gentle smile, "I never asked you to move the rock. I only asked you to push it, which you have faithfully done. Consider how you have grown and become strong. Think of those who saw your faithfulness and were encouraged to take on hard tasks in my name. Well done, my servant. Now, I will move the rock."

God's servants can honor Him wherever they attend college. They simply must be committed to the task.

---

234 Friesen, *Decision Making and the Will of God*, 171 ("If [God's] moral will has not been violated, there has been no sin. If there has been no sin, there should be no guilt").

CHAPTER 18

FINAL THOUGHTS

This has been an extremely difficult book for me to write. I attended public schools growing up and I obtained degrees from two liberal public universities for my undergraduate and graduate education (University of California at Santa Barbara and UCLA School of Law). Although two of my children started off at Christian schools, we moved them to well-regarded public schools when we had the chance. Only when I went back to school part-time as an adult to study biblical counseling at a purposefully Christian college did it become apparent to me what I had been missing. While there is no doubt that God has used my public education for good, there *is* a difference between the two experiences. My adult studies have opened my eyes to a different way of being educated, according to Scripture and through the lens of Scripture. In fact, prior to writing this book I likely would have joined many fellow Christians in their defensiveness about attending secular schools. As one stated to me when I asked about his decision to send his son to a secular school, "After all, you went to public schools and you turned out just fine." However, the fact that I turned out "just fine" in the world's eyes is not the test. The point is that even in our freedom as believers, some decisions are just *better* than others. In looking back—and in light of the in-depth study of Scripture this book has compelled me to undertake—I do wonder how much more I could have grown or been used in the kingdom had I sat at the feet of professors who knew and loved God and who desired the same for me.

But I do not reside in the past, nor can I worry about how some might receive the counsel set forth in this book. In the words of Paul, "one thing I do: forgetting what lies behind and straining forward to what lies ahead, I press on toward the goal for the prize of the upward call of God in Christ Jesus. Let those of us who are mature think this way" (Philippians 3:13-15). The goals are clear. Every believer should seek to grow into a fully mature Christian (Colossians 1:28; Ephesians

4:13; 2 Timothy 2:15). Likewise, every believer must "Look carefully then how you walk, not as unwise but as wise, making the best use of the time, because the days are evil. Therefore do not be foolish, but understand what the will of the Lord is" (Ephesians 5:15-17). If believers seek God, they will find Him (Matthew 6:33).

As to this point, I recently was in an airport with a law firm colleague of mine who asked me what I was reading. Before I could answer, he said, "It's not something religious again, is it? You should expand your horizons." I queried back to him, "How can I expand my horizons beyond an infinite God?" The conversation fizzled as he stuck his nose back into his *Sports Illustrated* magazine, which was already obsolete by the time it had hit the newsstand.

This conversation reminded me that my unbelieving friend is blind to the things of God, to the beauty, riches, and grace God offers, and even to the wisdom and benefit of seeking God with all of one's might (Isaiah 44:18; 1 Corinthians 2:14; 2 Corinthians 4:4). And it further reminded me that without God's grace, I, too, would be blind (1 Corinthians 15:10). However, because God has redeemed me through the blood of Jesus and has forgiven me of my sins (Ephesians 1:7), I can dig joyfully through His Word and, in awe, counsel others to do the same in every moment and for every decision. After all, even though my soul clings to Him, it is God's right hand that upholds me (Psalm 63:8). And that, my friends, should be enough to make every believer passionate about knowing and serving God—even in the college years. Choose well.

BIBLIOGRAPHY

Adams, Jay. *A Theology of Christian Counseling*. Grand Rapids, MI: Zondervan, 1986.

Alcorn, Randy. "Choosing a Christian College or Secular University." *Eternal Perspectives Ministries*. Accessed April 16, 2015. http://www.epm.org/blog/2009/Aug/19/question-and-answer-of-the-week-choosing-a-christi.

———. *Money, Possessions, and Eternity*. Carol Stream, IL: Tyndale House Publishers, Inc., 1989.

———. *The Treasure Principle*. Sisters, OR: Multnomah Publishers, Inc. 2001.

Amondson, Katie Browness. "50 Colleges and Universities with the Happiest Freshmen." *College Choice*. Accessed December 31, 2014. http://www.collegechoice.net/posts/colleges-with-happiest-freshman/.

Anderson-Lopez, Kristen and Robert Lopez. "Let it Go." *Frozen: The Songs*. Disney, 2014. CD.

Asher, Marshall and Mary. *The Christian's Guide to Psychological Terms*. Bemidji, MN: Focus Publishing, 2004.

Associated Press. "Ireland backs legalizing gay marriage by a landslide." *Fox News*. Accessed September 15, 2015. http://www.foxnews.com/world/2015/05/23/ireland-gay-marriage/.

Astin, Alexander and Helen Astin. "Spirituality in Higher Education: Study Reveals Influences of College on Students' Spiritual and Religious Development." *Spirituality.UCLA.edu*. Higher Education Research Institute. Accessed January 30, 2016. http://spirituality.ucla.edu/docs/news/release_college_experience.pdf.

Astin, Alexander and Helen Astin and Jennifer Lindholm. *Cultivating the Spirit: How College Can Enhance Students' Inner Lives*. San Francisco, CA: John Wiley & Sons, Inc., 2011.

Baylor University. "Christian Commitment." *Baylor.edu*. Accessed August 27, 2015. http://www.baylor.edu/about/index.php?id=88782.

Bennett, Jessica. "Northwestern University's Live Sex Class." *The Daily Beast.* Accessed September 14, 2015. http://www.thedailybeast.com/articles/2011/03/03/the-story-behind-northwestern-universitys-live-sex-class.html.

Big Future. "College: What It's All About and Why it Matters." *College Board.* Accessed January 30, 2016. https://bigfuture.collegeboard.org/get-started/know-yourself/college-what-its-all-about-and-why-it-matters.

Blamires, Harry. *The Christian Mind.* London: Holy Trinity Church, 1963.

Bonomi, Patricia. *Under the Cope of Heaven: Religion, Society, and Politics in Colonial America.* New York: Oxford University Press, 1986.

Boston University Student Health Services. "Frisky February: 28 Days of Stimulation." *Boston University.* Accessed September 14, 2015. http://www.bu.edu/shs/wellness/wellness-programs/sexual/frisky-february-events/.

Bridges, Jerry. *Respectable Sins.* Colorado Springs, CO: NavPress, 2007.

Briody, Blaire. "11 Public Universities with the Worst Graduation Rates." *The Fiscal Times.* Accessed November 10, 2014. http://www.thefiscaltimes.com/Articles/2012/05/17/11-Public-Universities-with-the-Worst-Graduation-Rates.

Brown, Bill. "Top 10 Challenges Christian Students Face in College." *Cedarville University.* Accessed September 22, 2015. https://www.cedarville.edu/eNews/ParentPrep/2012/Challenges-Christian-Students-Face-in-College.aspx.

Bunyan, John. *Pilgrim's Progress (in Today's English).* Retold by James Thomas. Chicago, IL: Moody Publishers, 1992.

Butler, Jack. "College Offers Course Devoted Entirely to Pornography." *The College Fix.* Accessed September 17, 2015. http://www.thecollegefix.com/post/13039/.

Bibliography

Calvin, John. *Commentary on the Book of Psalms.* Translated by James Anderson. Grand Rapids, MI: Wm. B. Eerdmans Publishing Company, 1948.

Challies, Tim. "Sanctification is a Community Project." Citing Mike Bullmore. *Challies.Com.* Accessed October 6, 2015. http://www.challies.com/ christian-living/sanctification-is-a-community-project.

Chediak, Alex. *Preparing Your Teen for College.* Carol Stream, IL: Tyndale House Publishers, Inc., 2014.

Clydesdale, Tim. "Abandoned, Pursued, or Safely Stowed? The Religious Life of First Year Undergraduates." Social Science Research Council Essay, October 9, 2006. Cited in Fuller Youth Institute. "You Make the Call: What College Freshmen Need to Hear from their Youth Pastors." *Sticky Faith.* Accessed September 22, 2015. http://stickyfaith.org/articles/you-make-the-call.

Cobb, McKinley. "Teen Dreams: Church Influences Career Choice." *Crosswalk. com.* Accessed January 30, 2016. http://www.crosswalk.com/family/ parenting/teens/teenage-dreams.html.

College Board. 2016 *Book of Majors.* Edited by Tom Vanderberg. New York: Guidance Publications, 2015.

College Data. "What's the Price Tag for a College Education?" *College Data*.com. Accessed May 1, 2015. http://www.collegedata.com/cs/content/content_ payarticle_tmpl.jhtml?articleId=10064.

Croft, Scott. "Biblical Dating: How It's Different from Modern Dating." *Boundless.* Accessed September 30, 2015. http://www.boundless.org/ relationships/2012/biblical-dating-how-its-different-from-modern-dating.

Cunningham, Conor. "Theology Must Save Science From Naturalism." *Religion and Ethics.* Accessed October 31, 2014. http://www.abc.net.au/religion/ articles/2012/05/22/3508607.htm.

Cusumano, Katherine. "The Truth Laid Bare: Naked Donut Run Sweetens Reading Period." *The Brown Daily Herald.* Accessed October 5, 2015. http://www. browndailyherald.com/2013/01/23/the-truth-laid-bare-naked-donut-run-sweetens-reading-period/.

Delitzsch, Franz. *Biblical Commentary on the Psalms*. Edinburgh: Morrison and Gibb, 1892.

Dennett, Daniel. *Darwin's Dangerous Idea*. New York: Simon & Schuster 1995.

Derrick, J.C. "Two Schools Leave CCCU—For Opposite Reasons." *WorldMag. org*. Accessed January 26, 2016. http://www.worldmag.com/2015/12/ two_schools_leave_cccu_for_opposite_reasons.

d'Escoto, David. "Is it a Sin to Send Our Kids to Public School?" *WND Commentary*. Accessed April 15, 2015. http://www.wnd. com/2009/06/102269/#.

Dionisopolous, Timothy. "Montana State University Set to Host 'Latex and Lace Condom Fashion Show,'" *Campus Reform*. Accessed October 5, 2015. http://campusreform.org/?ID=5376.

Edelen, William. "The Bible and the Gullible." *Infidels.org*. Accessed January 28, 2016. http://infidels.org/kiosk/article/the-bible-and-the-gullible-703.html.

Fitzgerald, Kersley. "What is the Purpose of College?" *Blogos*. Accessed September 15, 2015. http://www.blogos.org/thetakeaway/what-is-the-purpose-of-college.html.

Fortenbury, John. "The Christian Decision: Attend a Christian or Secular College?" *USA Today*. Accessed April 15, 2015. http://college.usatoday. com/2012/09/13/the-christian-decision-attend-a-christian-or-secular-college/.

Fox News. "College Prof Makes Students Recite Anti-American 'Pledge of Allegiance." *Fox News*. Accessed September 14, 2015. http://www. foxnews.com/us/2014/12/08/college-prof-makes-students-recite-anti-american-pledge-allegiance/.

Fox News. "University of California offers six choices for 'gender identity.'" *Fox News*. Accessed September 15, 2015. http://www.foxnews.com/ us/2015/07/28/university-california-offers-six-choices-for-gender-identity/?intcmp=hpbt3.

Bibliography

French, David. "Conservatives Have the Ability to Fight the University Left, So Let's Do It." *National Review.* Accessed November 12, 2015. http://www.nationalreview.com/article/426976/higher-education-reform-universities-left.

Friesen, Gary. *Decision Making and the Will of God.* Portland, OR: Multnomah Press, 1980.

Fuller Youth Institute. "You Make the Call: What College Freshmen Need to Hear from their Youth Pastors." *Sticky Faith.* Accessed September 22, 2015. http://stickyfaith.org/articles/you-make-the-call.

Gerrish, Brian. *A Prince of the Church: Schleiermacher and the Beginnings of Modern Theology.* Philadelphia: Fortress Press, 1984.

Gibson, David. "San Francisco Archbishop Salvatore Cordileone's Sad (But Predictable) Views on Caitlyn Jenner." *Huffington Post.* Accessed June 4, 2015. http://www.huffingtonpost.com/2015/06/04/salvatore-cordileone-gender-ideology_n_7507638.html.

Gilkerson, Luke. "Porn 101: College Campuses Using Porn in the Classroom. *Covenant Eyes.* Accessed September 17, 2015. http://www.covenanteyes.com/2008/10/31/porn-101-college-campuses-using-porn-in-the-classroom/.

Golden, Steve. "Creation on Campus." *Answers.* October-December 2014.

Got Questions Ministries. "What does it mean for a Christian to grow in the faith?" *GotQuestions.org.* Accessed April 17, 2015. http://www.gotquestions.org/Christian-grow-faith.html.

Grudem, Wayne. *Systematic Theology.* Grand Rapids, MI: Zondervan, 1994.

Ham, Ken. "Ken Ham Praises John MacArthur's Master's College for Leaving Association That Rejects Biblical Creation." *Worldview Weekend.* Accessed January 26, 2016. http://www.worldviewweekend.com/news/article/ken-ham-praises-john-macarthurs-masters-college-leaving-association-rejects-biblical.

Hansen, Collin. "The Holy and the Ivy." *Christianity Today.* Accessed April 13, 2015. http://www.christianitytoday.com/ct/2005/september/26.64.html?start=5.

Hanson, Victor David. "The Regrettable Decline of Higher Learning." *National Review.* Accessed February 6, 2016. http://www.nationalreview.com/article/430739/college-campus-safe-spaces-speech-codes-decline.

Hardgrove, Caitlin. "Top College Traditions to do before you Graduate." *Her Campus.* Accessed September 15, 2015. http://www.hercampus.com/life/top-college-traditions-do-you-graduate.

Harris, Alex and Brett Harris. *Do Hard Things.* Colorado Springs, CO: Multnomah Books, 2008.

Henderson, Steve. "Investing in Their Faith." *Christian College Guide.* Accessed April 16, 2015. http://www.christiancollegeguide.net/article/Investing-in-Their-Faith?page=2.

Henry, Matthew. *Matthew Henry's Commentary on the Whole Bible: Complete and Unabridged in One Volume.* Peabody, MA: Hendrickson Publishing, 1994.

Hoffman, Shirl James. "Sports Fanatics: How Christians have succumbed to the sports culture—and what might be done about it." *Christianity Today.* Accessed June 20, 2015. http://www.christianitytoday.com/ct/2010/february/sports-fanatics-football-shirl-hoffman.html.

Horton, Michael. "The Gospel and the Sufficiency of Scripture." *Modern Reformation.* Accessed July 19, 2013. http://www.modernreformation.org/default.php?page=articledisplay&var1=ArtRead&var2=1191&var3=.

Hua, Cynthia. "Sex Week Planned for February." *Yale Daily News.* Accessed September 14, 2015. http://yaledailynews.com/blog/2012/12/12/sex-week-planned-for-february/.

Humphrey, Nick. "What Shall We Tell the Children?" Amnesty Lecture. Oxford, February 21, 1997. Accessed September 17, 2015. https://www.youtube.com/watch?v=yfr6SkaBuq0.

Jamieson, Robert, A. R. Fausset, and David Brown. *Commentary Critical and Explanatory on the Whole Bible*, vol. 1. Oak Harbor, WA: Logos Research Systems, Inc., 1997.

Jarrett, Gregg. "What are college professors (not) teaching?" *Fox News*. Accessed September 15, 2015. http://www.foxnews.com/opinion/2014/10/14/what-are-college-professors-not-teaching/?intcmp=features.

Johnson, Phillip. Foreword to *Total Truth*, by Nancy Pearcey, 11-13. Wheaton, IL: Crossway Books, 2005.

Keathley III, J. Hampton. "Psalm 1: Two Ways of Life—A Psalm of Wisdom." *Bible.org*. Accessed March 16, 2015. https://bible.org/article/psalm-1-two-ways-life-psalm-wisdom.

Kelly, Brian. "Is College Still Worth It?" *U.S. News & World Report*. September 2010.

Kiley, Kevin. "Thumbing through the Napoleonic Wars: The Words of Napoleon and Others Who May Have Influenced His Methods." *The Napoleon Series*. Accessed October 5, 2015. http://www.napoleon-series.org/research/napoleon/c_quotes.html.

Koukl, Greg. "Augustine on Evil." *Stand to Reason*. Accessed October 5, 2015. http://www.str.org/articles/augustine-on-evil#.VLNZ8otyc20.

Kuyper, Abraham. "Abraham Kuyper Quotes." *Good Reads*. Accessed October 6, 2015. http://www.goodreads.com/quotes/17308-he-is-your-friend-who-pushes-you-nearer-to-god.

———. "Abraham Kuyper Quotes." *Good Reads*. Accessed October 7, 2015. https://www.goodreads.com/quotes/843713-whatever-man-may-stand-whatever-he-may-do-to-whatever.

Lambert, Heath. "The Sufficiency of Scripture." *Biblical Counseling Coalition*. Accessed July 23, 2013. http://biblicalcounselingcoalition.org/blogs/2012/06/18/the-sufficiency-of-scripture/.

———. "Theological Basis of Biblical Counseling II." Lecture, The Master's College, Santa Clarita, California, July 23, 2013.

Larson, Steven. "Duke Approves Gender-Neutral Housing for Freshman to Accommodate LGBTQAI Students." *Campus Reform*. Accessed October 5, 2015. http://campusreform.org/?ID=5367.

Leahy, Michael. *Porn University: What college students are really saying about sex on campus*. Chicago, IL: Northfield Publishing, 2009.

Lemmel, Helen. "Turn Your Eyes Upon Jesus." *Timeless Truths*. Accessed October 5, 2015. http://library.timelesstruths.org/music/Turn_Your_Eyes_upon_Jesus/ (public domain, 1922).

Leo, John. "Professors Who See No Evil." *Aish.com*. Accessed September 16, 2015. http://www.aish.com/sp/ph/48923192.html.

Lewis, C.S. *God in the Dock: Essays on Theology and Ethics*. Edited by Walter Hooper. Grand Rapids, MI: Eerdmans Publishing Company, 1970.

———. *The Weight of Glory*. New York: The MacMillan Company, 1949.

Lickerman, Alex. "The True Meaning of Friendship." *Psychology Today*. Accessed August 26, 2015. https://www.psychologytoday.com/blog/happiness-in-world/201312/the-true-meaning-friendship.

Link, E.G. "How Much is Enough?" *Stewardship Ministries*. Accessed April 8, 2015. http://www.stewardshipministries.org/blog/2012/03/01/how-much-is-enough/.

Lisle, Jason. "Surviving Secular College." *Answers in Genesis*. Accessed September 23, 2015. https://answersingenesis.org/college/surviving-secular-college/.

MacArthur, John. "Do Adults Still Need to Obey Their Parents?" *Grace to* You. Accessed September 23, 2015. https://www.gty.org/resources/bible-qna/ BQ082212/do-adults-still-need-to-obey-their-parents.

———. "How to Study Your Bible." *Grace to You.* Accessed March 9, 2015. http://www.gty.org/resources/positions/P16/how-to-study-your-bible?term=Psalm 1:1.

———. "Embracing the Authority and Sufficiency of Scripture." In *Think Biblically.* Edited by John MacArthur. Wheaton, IL: Crossway, 2003.

———. "Introduction." In *Think Biblically.* Edited by John MacArthur. Wheaton, IL: Crossway, 2003.

———. "John MacArthur on Choosing a College." *The Master's College.* Accessed April 13, 2015. https://www.youtube.com/ watch?v=zGJ7vaFD5Oc.

———. "MacArthur on Education—Proper Education." *The Master's College.* Accessed July 28, 2015. https://www.youtube.com/watch?v=Qjx-hVbcgDA.

———. *Rediscovering Expository Preaching.* Dallas, TX: Word Publishing, 1992.

———. "Separating from Unbelievers, Part I." Sermon, Grace Community Church, Sun Valley, CA, July 23, 1995.

———. *Strange Fire.* Nashville, TN: Nelson Books, 2013.

———. "The Essentials of Handling God's Word, Part 3." Sermon, Grace Community Church, Sun Valley, CA, February 22, 2015.

———. "Through them…to the World." *The Master's College.* Accessed August 5, 2015. http://www.masters.edu/media/banner/education-2015/.

———. "We will not bow." *Grace to You.* Accessed September 28, 2015. http:// www.gty.org/resources/sermons/80-425/we-will-not-bow.

————. "What is Biblical Discernment and Why is it Important?" *Grace to You*. Accessed January 19, 2015. http://www.gty.org/resources/questions/QA138/What-is-biblical-discernment-and-why-is-it-important.

Mack, Wayne. *Homework Manual for Biblical Living*. Phillipsburg, NJ: P&R Publishing, 1979.

Mayhue, Richard. "The Authority of Scripture." *The Master's Seminary Journal*, 15/2 (Fall 2004).

McCallum, Dennis. "Five Worldviews." *Xenos Christian Fellowship*. Accessed January 6, 2015. http://www.xenos.org/classes/papers/5wldview.htm.

McDaniel, Chip. *The English-Hebrew Reverse Interlinear Old Testament English Standard Version*. Lexham Press, 2009.

McGinnis, KC. "6 Ways to Waste Your College Education." *Relevant Magazine*. Accessed April 15, 2015. http://www.relevantmagazine.com/relevant-u/undergrad/6-ways-waste-your-college-education.

Miller, Patricia and Keith. *Quick Scripture Reference for Counseling Youth*. Grand Rapids, MI: Baker Books, 2006.

Milton, John. *Tractate on Education*. Vol. III, Part 4. In *The Harvard Classics*. New York: P.F. Collier & Son, 1909-1914. Accessed September 17, 2015. http://www.bartleby.com/3/4/1.html.

Mitchell, Tommy. "Should Creation Be Taught in Public Schools?" *Answers*. October-December 2014.

Moore, T.M. "Ease and Indulgence." *The Chuck Colson Center for Christian Worldview*. Accessed April 21, 2015. http://www.colsoncenter.org/the-center/columns/worldview-bible/22817-ease-and-indulgence.

————. "Losing your way on the path to wisdom." *The Chuck Colson Center for Christian Worldview*. Accessed April 21, 2015. http://www.colsoncenter.org/the-center/columns/viewpoint/22810-losing-your-way-on-the-path-to-wisdom.

Bibliography

Morse, Robert. "Freshmen Students Say Rankings Aren't Key Factor in College Choice: Academic reputation tops the list of reasons students choose a college." *U.S. News & World Report.* Accessed December 31, 2014. http://www.usnews.com/education/blogs/college-rankings-blog/2013/01/31/freshmen-students-say-rankings-arent-key-factor-in-college-choice.

Neander, Joachim. "Praise to the Lord, the Almighty." *Timeless Truths.* Accessed October 5, 2015. http://library.timelesstruths.org/music/Praise_to_the_Lord_the_Almighty/ (public domain, 1680).

Nelson, Richard William. "Darwin Then and Now." *DarwinThenandNow.com.* Accessed January 29, 2016. http://www.darwinthenandnow.com/2010/08/butterfly-nightmare/.

Newlon, Cara. "College Students Still Often Find Spouses on Campus." *USA Today.* Accessed September 30, 2015. http://www.usatoday.com/story/news/nation/2013/10/15/college-marriage-facebook/2989039/.

Nichols, James Michael. "Harvard University Offers 'What What In The Butt: Anal Sex 101.'" *Huffington Post.* Accessed October 5, 2015. http://www.huffingtonpost.com/2014/11/05/harvard-anal-sex-class_n_6102804.html.

Osler, Mark. "The 5 Scariest Teachings of Jesus." *The Huffington Post.* Accessed September 15, 2015. http://www.huffingtonpost.com/mark-osler/scariest-teachings-of-jesus_b_6075490.html?ncid=txtlnkusaolp00000592.

Osteen, Joel. *Your Best Life Now.* New York: FaithWords, 2004.

O'Toole, Garson. "Do not be so open-minded that your brains fall out." *Quote Investigator.* Accessed September 25, 2015. http://quoteinvestigator.com/2014/04/13/open-mind/.

Owen, John. *Of The Mortification of Sin in Believers* (1656). In *Overcoming Sin & Temptation.* Edited by Kelly Kapic and Justin Taylor. Wheaton, IL: Crossway Books, 2006.

Payne, J. Barton. "Higher Criticism and Biblical Inerrancy." In *Inerrancy*. Edited by Norman Geisler. Grand Rapids, MI: Zondervan Publishing House, 1980.

Peace, Martha. *The Excellent Wife*. Bemidji, MN: Focus Publishing, 1995.

Pearcey, Nancy. *Total Truth*. Wheaton, IL: Crossway Books, 2005.

Pennell, Julie. "What College Students Really Think About Feminism." *Teen Vogue*. Accessed July 13, 2015. https://www.yahoo.com/style/what-college-students-really-think-about-feminism-123750899955.html.

Piper, John. "Thoughts on the Sufficiency of Scripture: What it does and doesn't mean." *Desiring God Ministries*. Accessed July 19, 2013. http://www.desiringgod.org/resource-library/taste-see-articles/thoughts-on-the-sufficiency-of-scripture.

Plato. *Republic, Book VII*. Translated by Benjamin Jowett (1892). Annotated by David Trumbull. Agathan Associates 2009. Accessed October 6, 2015. http://www.bostonleadershipbuilders.com/plato/republic/book8.htm.

Postman, Neil. *The Disappearance of Childhood*. New York: Delacorte Press, 1982.

Prince, David. "Are youth sports a friend or foe of Christian discipleship?" *The Ethics and Religious Liberties Convention of the Southern Baptist Convention*. Accessed June 20, 2015. https://erlc.com/article/are-youth-sports-a-friend-or-foe-of-christian-discipleship.

Julie and Stephanie Kafka. "Life in College Matters for Life after College." *Gallup*. Accessed January 28, 2016. http://www.gallup.com/poll/168848/life-college-matters-life-college.aspx.

Riggs, Mike, and Carolyn Riggs. *The Trojan Horse in Christian Education: A survey of contributing thought trends*. Castaic, California: Lamp & Quill International, 2006.

Ross, Allen P. "Psalms," in *The Bible Knowledge Commentary: An Exposition of the Scriptures*, vol. 1. Edited by J. F. Walvoord and R. B. Zuck. Wheaton, IL: Victor Books, 1985.

Ryle, J.C. "The Duties of Parents." WholesomeWords.org. Accessed March 12, 2015. http://www.wholesomewords.org/etexts/ryle/ryleduties.pdf. First published in *The Upper Room: Being Truths for the Times*. London: William Hunt & Co., 1888.

Samples, Kenneth. "What in the World is a Worldview?" *Reasons to Believe.* Accessed January 6, 2015. http://www.reasons.org/articles/what-in-the-world-is-a-worldview.

Schweitzer, Albert. *Albert Schweitzer: Thoughts for Our Times.*" Ed. Erica Anderson. Mount Vernon, NY: The Peter Pauper Press, 1975.

Seagren, Thom. "Christian Colleges v. Secular Colleges: What's the Difference?" *The Christian Connector, Inc.* Accessed April 15, 2015. http://www. christianconnector.com/Christian-college-tips/Selecting-Best-College-Christian-vs-Secular.cfm.

Seaton, George, dir. *Miracle on 34th Street*. Twentieth Century Fox Film Corporation, 1947. DVD. 20th Century Fox Home Entertainment, 2006.

Selderhuis, Herman. *Calvin's Theology of the Psalms*. Grand Rapids, MI: Baker Academic, 2007.

Sexual Empowerment and Awareness. "Schedule: Sex Week at University of Texas." *SexweekUT.org.* Accessed November 10, 2014. http://sexweekut. org/schedule/.

Sexual Health Education & Advocacy throughout Harvard College. "Sex Week at Harvard." *Hsexweek.org.* Accessed October 5, 2015. http://www. hsexweek.org/schedule/.

Sims, Ruth. "New research on student emotions in college choice: Part 1." *Noel-Levitz.* Accessed December 31, 2014. http://blog.noellevitz. com/2014/08/28/new-research-student-emotions-college-choice-part-1/.

Sire, James. "8 Questions Every Worldview Must Answer." *Christianity.com*. Accessed January 6, 2015. http://www.christianity.com/theology/other-religions-beliefs/8-questions-every-worldview-must-answer.html?p=0.

Spence-Jones, H.D.M., ed. *2 Timothy*. The Pulpit Commentary. London: Funk & Wagnalls Company, 1909.

———. *Psalms*. The Pulpit Commentary. London: Funk & Wagnalls Company, 1909.

Spurgeon, Charles. "The Treasury of David: Psalm 1." *The Spurgeon Archive*. Accessed March 13, 2015. http://www.spurgeon.org/treasury/ps001.htm.

Stevenson, Richard Taylor. *John Calvin the Statesman*. New York: Jennings & Graham, 1907.

Stoffel, Brian. "Here's How Much the Typical American Made Last Year, By Age and Sex -- How Do You Compare?" *The Motley Fool*. Accessed May 1, 2015. http://www.fool.com/investing/general/2015/03/02/heres-how-much-the-typical-american-made-last-ye-2.aspx.

Stonestreet, John and Chuck Edwards. "Students Abandoning the Faith." *Summit Ministries*. Accessed October 7, 2015. http://www.summit.org/resources/essays/students-abandoning-the-faith/.

Street, John. "Why Biblical Counseling and Not Psychology?" In *Think Biblically*. Edited by John MacArthur. Wheaton, IL: Crossway, 2003.

Templeton, Michael. "The 50 Best Christian Colleges in the U.S." *Christian Universities Online*. Accessed August 27, 2015. http://www.christianuniversitiesonline.org/best-christian-colleges/.

The Westminster Confession of Faith. 3rd ed. Lawrenceville, GA: Committee for Christian Education and Publications, 1990.

Timpf, Katherine. "University of Arizona class requires students to participate in 'Condom Olympics'." *Campus Reform*. Accessed October 5, 2015. http://campusreform.org/?ID=5437.

————. "Despite protest, women's college refuses to remove realistic statue of man sleepwalking in his underwear." *Campus Reform*. Accessed October 5, 2015. http://campusreform.org/?ID=5421.

————. "Students film feminist porno in Columbia University library." *Campus Reform*. Accessed October 5, 2015. http://campusreform.org/?ID=5414.

————. "U of Chicago to host 'clothing optional' dance party in campus hall." *Campus Reform*. Accessed October 5, 2015. http://campusreform.org/?ID=5403.

————. "Northwestern Univ. College Feminists celebrated Sex Week with 'sex position cookies.'" *Campus Reform*. Accessed October 5, 2015. http://campusreform.org/?ID=5369.

————. "Public university Sex Week to teach masturbation, when orgasms are a 'political act'." *Campus Reform*. Accessed October 5, 2015. http://www.campusreform.org/?ID=5397.

————. "Public university spending at least $25,500 on Sex Week." *Campus Reform*. Accessed October 5, 2015. http://campusreform.org/?ID=5413.

Tocqueville, Alexis de. *Democracy in America*. Vol. 2. New York: J. & H. G. Langley, 1840.

Tozer, A.W. *Man: The Dwelling Place of God*. In *Gems from Tozer*. Harrisburg, PA: Christian Publications, Inc., 1969.

————. *The Knowledge of the Holy*. New York: HarperCollins Publishers Inc., 1961.

————. *The Pursuit of God*. Camp Hill, PA: Christian Publications, Inc., 1982.

Tripp, Ted. *Shepherding a Child's Heart*. Wapwallopen, PA: Shepherd Press, 2005.

UCLA Art & Global Health Center. "UCLA Sex Squad." *Artglobalhealth. org*. Accessed September 14, 2015. http://artglobalhealth.org/amp/uclasexsquad/.

Unseth, Christopher. "3 Reasons Christians Should Consider a Non-Christian College." *Relevant Magazine*. Accessed April 15, 2015. http://www. relevantmagazine.com/relevant-u/undergrad/3-reasons-christians-should-attend-non-christian-college#comments.

U.S. Census Bureau. "The Big Payoff: Educational Attainment and Synthetic Estimates of Work-Life Earnings." *U.S. Department of Commerce*. Accessed April 2, 2015. https://www.census.gov/prod/2002pubs/p23-210. pdf.

Veith, Gene. *Loving God With All Your Mind*. Wheaton, IL: Crossway, 1987.

Vo, Lam Thy. "What Americans Earn." *Planet Money*. Accessed May 1, 2015. http://www.npr.org/blogs/money/2012/07/16/156688596/what-americans-earn.

Watts, Isaac. "When I Survey The Wonderous Cross." *Timeless Truths*. Accessed October 5, 2015. http://library.timelesstruths.org/music/When_I_Survey_the_Wondrous_Cross/ (public domain, 1707).

Welch, Ed. "When Scripture Seems Silent." *CCEF*. Accessed March 30, 2015. http://www.ccef.org/resources/blog/when-scripture-seems-silent.

Welland, Colin. *Chariots of Fire*. Warner Bros. Pictures, 1981. DVD. Warner Home Video, 1992.

Wesley, John. "The Use of Money, Sermon 50." *Wesley Center Online*. Accessed October 5, 2015. http://wesley.nnu.edu/john-wesley/the-sermons-of-john-wesley-1872-edition/sermon-50-the-use-of-money/.

White, James. *Scripture Alone*. Minneapolis, MN: Bethany House, 2004.

White, John. "Secular Enslavement," in *What Does the Lord Require of You?* Ed. Lynn R. Buzzard. Beaver Falls, PA: Geneva School of Law, 1997.

Wiesletier, Leon. "The Iran Deal and the Rut of History." *The Atlantic*. Accessed July 27, 2015. http://www.theatlantic.com/international/archive/2015/07/iran-deal-history/399644/.

Will, George. "The Speech Every 2015 College Grad Needs to Hear." *Prager University.* Accessed August 4, 2015. http://www.prageruniversity.com/ Life-Studies/The-Speech-Every-2015-College-Grad-Needs-to-Hear.html.

Wilson, Douglas. "Biologs, Respectability, and Classical Christian Education." *Blog and Mablog.* Accessed May 27, 2015. http://dougwils.com/s7-engaging-the-culture/biologos-respectability-and-classical-christian-education.html.

————. "Parenting Young People I." *Blog and Mablog.* Accessed October 7, 2015. http://dougwils.com/s8-expository/parenting-young-people-i.html.

————. "Scripture Forbids Us to Educate Our Children in the Public Schools." *Center for Reformed Theology and Apologetics.* Accessed September 28, 2015. http://www.reformed.org/webfiles/antithesis/index. html?mainframe=/webfiles/antithesis/v2n1/ant_v2n1_issue1.htm.

————. *Standing on the Promises.* Moscow, ID: Canon Press, 1997.

————. *Why Christian Kids Need a Christian Education.* Monroe, LA: Athanasius Press, 2013.

Wilson, Gerald. *The NIV Application Commentary: Psalms - Vol. 1.* Grand Rapids, MI: Zondervan, 2002.

Wolfe, Tom. *I am Charlotte Simmons.* New York: Farrar, Straus and Giroux, 2004.

Wyer, Kathy. "Survey: More freshmen than ever say they go to college to get better jobs, make more money - The American Freshman: National Norms Fall 2012." *Higher Education Research Institute.* Accessed December 31, 2014. http://www.heri.ucla.edu/pr-display.php?prQry=111.

About the Author

Todd Sorrell is a certified biblical counselor with the Association of Certified Biblical Counselors (ACBC). He is an attorney, businessman, and author. He has spent over 20 years practicing law at one of the largest international law firms in the world, where he was the first lawyer since the opening of the Los Angeles office to rise through the ranks to be made full equity partner. His legal practice focuses on a wide variety of domestic and international civil disputes, where he handles jury and bench trials, mediations and arbitrations. Todd sometimes acts as an advocate and sometimes as a mediator, arbitrator, conciliator, or temporary judge.

Early in his legal career, Todd was named to the list of Southern California Rising Stars, and he repeatedly has been selected by his peers as a Southern California "Super Lawyer," an honor reserved for less than 5% of attorneys in the State. In addition, Todd has founded a number of successful businesses in varying industries. Todd holds degrees from the University of California at Santa Barbara (B.A. Spanish), The Master's University (Master of Arts in Biblical Counseling), and UCLA School of Law (J.D.).

Todd is certified through the Association of Certified Biblical Counselors, and he has taught courses on biblical conflict resolution and biblical counseling. He has written one other book, *Journey to the Bending Light*, which is a Christian allegory for youth. Todd lives in southern California with his wife Celia and their three children, where he is involved in his local church.

The College Choice